OPPOSING
VIEWPOINTS®
SERIES

The Federal Budget

Other Books of Related Interest:

Opposing Viewpoints Series

Alternative Lending

The Banking Crisis

Free Trade

Government Spending

At Issue Series

Campaign Finance

Should the Federal Budget Be Balanced?

Should the Federal Budget Bail Out Private Industry?

Current Controversies Series

Capitalism

Consumer Debt

Fair Trade

The U.S. Economy

"Congress shall make
no law ... abridging
the freedom of speech,
or of the press."

First Amendment to the U.S. Constitution

The basic foundation of our democracy is the First Amendment guarantee of freedom of expression. The Opposing Viewpoints Series is dedicated to the concept of this basic freedom and the idea that it is more important to practice it than to enshrine it.

OPPOSING VIEWPOINTS® SERIES

The Federal Budget

Amanda Hiber, Book Editor

GREENHAVEN PRESS
A part of Gale, Cengage Learning

GALE
CENGAGE Learning™

Detroit • New York • San Francisco • New Haven, Conn • Waterville, Maine • London

GALE
CENGAGE Learning

Christine Nasso, *Publisher*
Elizabeth Des Chenes, *Managing Editor*

© 2010 Greenhaven Press, a part of Gale, Cengage Learning.

Gale and Greenhaven Press are registered trademarks used herein under license.

For more information, contact:
Greenhaven Press
27500 Drake Rd.
Farmington Hills, MI 48331-3535
Or you can visit our Internet site at gale.cengage.com

For product information and technology assistance, contact us at

Gale Customer Support, 1-800-877-4253
For permission to use material from this text or product, submit all requests online at www.cengage.com/permissions

Further permissions questions can be emailed to permissionrequest@cengage.com

Articles in Greenhaven Press anthologies are often edited for length to meet page requirements. In addition, original titles of these works are changed to clearly present the main thesis and to explicitly indicate the author's opinion. Every effort is made to ensure that Greenhaven Press accurately reflects the original intent of the authors. Every effort has been made to trace the owners of copyrighted material.

Cover image copyright James Steidl, 2009. Used under license from Shutterstock.com.

LIBRARY OF CONGRESS CATALOGING-IN-PUBLICATION DATA

The federal budget / Amanda Hiber, book editor.
    p. cm. -- (Opposing viewpoints)
    Includes bibliographical references and index.
    978-0-7377-4769-0 (hardcover) -- ISBN 978-0-7377-4770-6 (pbk.)
    1. Budget--United States. I. Hiber, Amanda.
    HJ2051.F388 2010
    336.73--dc22
                                                2009048146

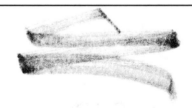

Printed in the United States of America
2 3 4 5 6 7 14 13 12 11 10

Contents

Chapter 1: How Effective Is the Current Federal Budget Process?

Chapter 2: How Do Federal Budget Deficits Affect the Nation's Economy?

Chapter 3: How Should Federal Budget Revenue Be Raised?

Chapter 4: How Should Federal Budget Money Be Spent?

Why Consider Opposing Viewpoints?

> *"The only way in which a human being can make some approach to knowing the whole of a subject is by hearing what can be said about it by persons of every variety of opinion and studying all modes in which it can be looked at by every character of mind. No wise man ever acquired his wisdom in any mode but this."*
>
> *John Stuart Mill*

In our media-intensive culture it is not difficult to find differing opinions. Thousands of newspapers and magazines and dozens of radio and television talk shows resound with differing points of view. The difficulty lies in deciding which opinion to agree with and which "experts" seem the most credible. The more inundated we become with differing opinions and claims, the more essential it is to hone critical reading and thinking skills to evaluate these ideas. Opposing Viewpoints books address this problem directly by presenting stimulating debates that can be used to enhance and teach these skills. The varied opinions contained in each book examine many different aspects of a single issue. While examining these conveniently edited opposing views, readers can develop critical thinking skills such as the ability to compare and contrast authors' credibility, facts, argumentation styles, use of persuasive techniques, and other stylistic tools. In short, the Opposing Viewpoints Series is an ideal way to attain the higher-level thinking and reading skills so essential in a culture of diverse and contradictory opinions.

In addition to providing a tool for critical thinking, Opposing Viewpoints books challenge readers to question their own strongly held opinions and assumptions. Most people form their opinions on the basis of upbringing, peer pressure, and personal, cultural, or professional bias. By reading carefully balanced opposing views, readers must directly confront new ideas as well as the opinions of those with whom they disagree. This is not to argue simplistically that everyone who reads opposing views will—or should—change his or her opinion. Instead, the series enhances readers' understanding of their own views by encouraging confrontation with opposing ideas. Careful examination of others' views can lead to the readers' understanding of the logical inconsistencies in their own opinions, perspective on why they hold an opinion, and the consideration of the possibility that their opinion requires further evaluation.

Evaluating Other Opinions

To ensure that this type of examination occurs, Opposing Viewpoints books present all types of opinions. Prominent spokespeople on different sides of each issue as well as well-known professionals from many disciplines challenge the reader. An additional goal of the series is to provide a forum for other, less known, or even unpopular viewpoints. The opinion of an ordinary person who has had to make the decision to cut off life support from a terminally ill relative, for example, may be just as valuable and provide just as much insight as a medical ethicist's professional opinion. The editors have two additional purposes in including these less known views. One, the editors encourage readers to respect others' opinions—even when not enhanced by professional credibility. It is only by reading or listening to and objectively evaluating others' ideas that one can determine whether they are worthy of consideration. Two, the inclusion of such viewpoints encourages the important critical thinking skill of objectively evaluating an author's credentials and bias. This evaluation will illuminate an author's reasons for taking a particular stance on an issue and will aid in readers' evaluation of the author's ideas.

It is our hope that these books will give readers a deeper understanding of the issues debated and an appreciation of the complexity of even seemingly simple issues when good and honest people disagree. This awareness is particularly important in a democratic society such as ours in which people enter into public debate to determine the common good. Those with whom one disagrees should not be regarded as enemies but rather as people whose views deserve careful examination and may shed light on one's own.

Thomas Jefferson once said that "difference of opinion leads to inquiry, and inquiry to truth." Jefferson, a broadly educated man, argued that "if a nation expects to be ignorant and free . . . it expects what never was and never will be." As individuals and as a nation, it is imperative that we consider the opinions of others and examine them with skill and discernment. The Opposing Viewpoints Series is intended to help readers achieve this goal.

David L. Bender and Bruno Leone,
Founders

Introduction

"If you really want to know what people value most, look at how they spend their money. This is true of individuals, households and whole nations."

Knight Kiplinger,
"Setting Our Priorities,"
Kiplinger.com, Jan. 28, 2008

When an individual spends money, he or she is making a choice, and this choice is, in large part, determined by what he or she holds dear. While the budget of a whole nation is certainly on a much higher scale than an individual's budget, it, too, reflects the values of those who inhabit the country, as well as the sacrifices they are willing to make. As Robert J. Samuelson states in a 2008 *Newsweek* article, "Budgets are not just numbers. They express political choices." In this way, the federal budget of the United States—including how money is spent *and* accumulated—can be said to mirror the nation's very identity.

In a 2005 *Christian Science Monitor* article, Pat M. Holt writes, "The budget is our main tool for allocating resources and setting national priorities and values." This is especially true when it comes to federal spending. The largest pieces of the fiscal year 2008 federal budget, for instance, were spent on defense and national security (21 percent of the budget) and Social Security (also 21 percent of the budget). The three major government health programs, Medicare, Medicaid, and the Children's Health Insurance Program (CHIP), make up another 20 percent. The other large pieces of the budget go to safety net programs (11 percent) and interest on debt (8 percent). All other spending—including transportation and infrastructure, scientific and medical research, and education—are taken from the remaining one-fifth of the federal budget. Many critics have deduced that, in spite of political rhetoric about the value of education, the United States does not actually place much value on education, given the amount spent on it (2 percent in fiscal year 2008).

The money a government spends on its priorities comes from its budget revenues—and, for most countries, these come primarily in the form of taxes. In fiscal year 2008, 60 percent of federal budget revenue came from taxes, most of it from income taxes. When citizens pay taxes, they are making a sacrifice for the good of their nation. So, just as spending reflects what a society values having, revenue reflects what the members of that society are willing to give up. Income tax rates in the United States are considerably lower than those of Western Europe. Ezra Klein writes in the *American Prospect* in 2009 that while the *highest* income tax rate in the United States is 35 percent, the income tax rate in the Netherlands is 52 percent. At the same time, Americans are somewhat notorious for complaining about the taxes they do pay. In a 2005 article in the same magazine, however, writers Robert Borosage and Celinda Lake argue that, "General attitudes on taxes [in the United States] are not as conservative as our political debate suggests." They go on to state, "In any discussion of priorities, a majority of Americans do not rate tax cuts first. . . . When [President George W.] Bush first made his case for tax cuts at a time of record budget surpluses, much of the public was skeptical. Polls suggested that people preferred investments in education and health care, or reducing the deficit to save Social Security, over tax cuts." For instance, Borosage and Lake write, "In the wake of September 11 and two wars, a solid majority of Americans (61 percent [versus] 34 percent) think that the taxes they pay are fair, according to a Gallup poll conducted in April [2005]. Consistent with other times in our history, these numbers reflect the dramatic way that war and national-security concerns influence public opinion." Indeed, during all other major wars, Americans were overwhelmingly willing to make economic (and other) sacrifices for the needs of their nation. While Americans' reluctance to pay taxes, and skepticism about how that tax money is spent, indicate our values, this readiness to sacrifice says something, too, about the U.S. national character.

In the same way that an individual's identity is ever shifting, so is a nation's; such shifts are evident in the history of the federal budget. For instance, in 2009 the United States was in the grip of a financial recession, with a national unemployment rate of over 9 percent, the highest rate in more than 25 years. Such conditions influenced both citizens' and lawmakers' priorities—and both called for more money allocated to helping out citizens in the short term, at the expense of reducing the federal deficit. It is reasonable to expect, however, that once the recession has ended, citizens and lawmakers alike will call for a reorienting of the budget to spend less money on helping citizens get back on their feet, and more on decreasing the federal deficit. The relationship between national priorities and the U.S. federal budget is evident throughout this book's chapters, "How Effective Is the Current Budget Process?"; "How Do Budget Deficits Affect the Nation's Economy?" "How Should Federal Budget Revenue Be Raised?" and "How Should Federal Budget Money Be Spent?" Understanding this relationship, and all its shifts and nuances, is key to comprehending the *hows* and *whys* of the nation's federal budget, as well as developing a greater understanding of the nation itself.

CHAPTER 1

How Effective Is the Current Federal Budget Process?

Chapter Preface

Many Americans may be surprised to learn that the current U.S. federal budget process was not prescribed by the Constitution; in fact, the Constitution did not prescribe a federal budget process at all. "The Constitution lists the power to lay and collect taxes and the power to borrow as powers of Congress," explains the Congressional Research Office (CRO) in a 2008 report. "The Constitution does not state how these legislative powers are to be exercised." An explicit budget system was deemed unnecessary, explains the report, "as long as the federal government was small and its spending and revenues were stable."

The process now used to generate a federal budget each fiscal year is primarily based in laws passed in the 20th century. According to the CRO report, "the incessant rise in federal spending and the recurrence of deficits" in the early part of that century "led Congress to seek a more coordinated means of making financial decisions." In response to this need, the Budget and Accounting Act of 1921 was passed. In a 1996 testimony given before the House Committee on the Budget, the Government Accountability Office (GAO) explains that this act "centralized power over executive agency budget requests under the President and—to balance this grant of power—moved control of the audit of spending from the Treasury to a new legislative branch entity, the GAO. The Congress also centralized its own spending decisions in the House and Senate Appropriations Committees." The CRO report describes the shift brought about by the 1921 law in more specific—and perhaps familiar—terms; under the new law, it says, "The President was required to submit his budget recommendations to Congress each year, and the Bureau of the Budget—renamed the Office of Management and Budget (OMB) in 1970—was created to assist him in carrying out his budgetary responsibilities."

After World War II, the CRO report explains, "some Members of Congress feared that dependence on the executive budget had bolstered the President's fiscal powers at the expense of Congress's; others felt that as long as its financial decisions were fragmented, Congress could not effectively control expenditures." In order to remedy these problems, many felt that Congress needed its own budget process. Finally, the 1974 Congressional Budget Act was passed, which, the CRO report says, "established a congressional budget process centered around a concurrent resolution on the budget, scheduled for adoption prior to legislative consideration of revenue or spending bills." The 1974 act also established the Congressional Budget Office (CBO).

Since the 1974 act, other important laws have been passed that have altered the budget process—including the Balanced Budget and Emergency Deficit Control Act of 1985, the Line Item Veto Act in 1996, and the Budget Enforcement Act of 1997, as well as others. The 1921 and 1974 acts are most significant in laying out the roles of the executive and legislative branches in the budget process, however—as well as how these two branches work together in the making of the federal budget. The ins and outs of this process, and its strengths and weaknesses, are vigorously debated in the following chapter.

> "Our current budget process is the prod-
> uct of several major reforms . . . but in
> recent times it has failed us in all the
> most important places."

The Federal Budget Process Should Be Reformed

Jim Bates

*Jim Bates is the project director for the Peterson-Pew Commis-
sion on Budget Reform at the Committee for a Responsible Federal Budget. In the following viewpoint, Bates argues that the
current federal budgetary process produces rushed, sloppy budgets. The budget process fails to produce a straightforward, realistic framework for the government's revenue or spending plans.
It also does not focus on long-term entitlement spending, the
biggest contributor to the federal deficit and debt. Last, enforcement rules in the current budget process are ineffective. The budget process must be reformed, Bates writes, to correct these and
other flaws.*

As you read, consider the following questions:

1. Why doesn't the budget resolution reflect the consensus
   of both the Legislative and Executive branches, according to Bates?

Jim Bates, "Fiscal Disorder," *The Ripon Forum*, vol. 43, Spring 2009. Copyright 2009, The
Ripon Forum. Reproduced by permission.

2. What "unlikely prediction" does Bates think the fiscal year 2008 federal budget made?

3. What does Bates feel the budget process should do to ensure that decisions aren't made that endanger the country's long-term fiscal health?

This past February [2009], four months after the beginning of the [2009] fiscal year, Congress passed the last bill needed to fund the government.

But what it finally passed was more than just late—it was sloppy. Instead of offering separate appropriation bills that could be debated thoughtfully and with undivided attention, Congress lumped them into one, gigantic 225-page "omnibus" bill and hurriedly passed it on the floor.

Does anyone think this bill got the scrutiny it deserved? Moreover, at a time of near-universal recognition that our entitlement [programs such as Social Security and Medicare] and tax policies are unsustainable, Congress has made no improvements in these areas for the next fiscal year. Our national conversation on this broken system is long overdue. And if we are serious about changing the situation, then budget reform will have to mean reforming the process by which Congress considers, passes, and evaluates its annual budget.

In theory, the federal budget process is straightforward.

First, the president submits his "budget," which is actually just a recommendation that reflects the administration's own priorities. After the president's budget, Congress creates a blueprint for itself called a budget resolution. This resolution is developed through the legislative process, but is not presented to the president and hence doesn't reflect the consensus of both the Congress and the Executive branches. What it is supposed to do is provide a framework for subsequent spending and tax bills. Congress then considers twelve separate appropriations bills, together with any tax and entitlement bills on its legislative agenda that will become law once they are signed by the President.

Our current budget process is the product of several major reforms—the last was in the 1970s—but in recent times it has failed us in all the most important places.

Current Process Is Unrealistic

The first—and most basic—criticism of the budget process is that it doesn't produce a simple, realistic framework for how government intends to spend in the short term, plan for entitlements, or impose taxes. The president's budget and Congress's budget resolution are both just preliminary steps in the passage of a budget. They can and often do get kicked aside in the scuffle between the appropriations, authorization, and tax writing committees, all of which create different pieces of legislation that combine to form the big fiscal picture.

Moreover, both the president's budget and the budget resolution make a variety of unrealistic assumptions that render them largely useless. For instance, the president's fiscal year 2008 budget accounted for negligible spending on the wars in Iraq and Afghanistan, and [it] made the unlikely prediction that Congress would soon allow expiring tax breaks to place billions of dollars in additional tax burden on the middle class.

Nor does the budget process focus efforts on the biggest drivers of deficits and the debt: long-term entitlement spending. Almost everyone knows that in the coming decades, we will be unable to sustain our entitlement commitments and tax policies, but the budget process doesn't focus on the level of entitlement growth in existing law or, for changes to existing entitlement law, growth that occurs outside of a narrow window of time. Existing budgetary limits are easily evaded by pushing policies outside this budget window or pretending that they will expire when they likely will not. In the end, most of Congress's time is spent on the 38 percent of the budget that makes up discretionary spending, with barely any formalized oversight on the mandatory side. . . .

What Budgets Are Supposed to Do

Step back for a moment and think about what budgets are supposed to do. We'd all like to spend as much as we want, but budgets show us our limits by bringing all of our obligations and revenue sources into one unified picture. An ideal budget would encourage policymakers to take a look at entitlement spending when they adjusted discretionary spending (and vice versa), weigh the importance of one tax break against other tax breaks, adjust revenue to compensate for new spending, and generally make real trade-offs across all categories.

The bottom line is that if something is important enough for the government to do, it is important enough to pay for either by raising taxes or cutting other spending. But our budget process is missing this fundamental connection between the parts. Instead, we foster compromise at the level of individual appropriations bills, where the question is simply how to spend money within a narrowly defined area of appropriations. In practice, lawmakers are actually encouraged to stick with their party when they vote on the budget resolution, but then vote with their districts or states when it comes to the appropriations bills.

Finally, the "teeth" of our budget process—enforcement— have proved themselves largely ineffective. The original pay-as-you-go rules had the force of law and were enforced by automatic spending cuts. The current rules are not legally binding and easily circumvented, whether through waving budget rules, designating phony emergencies, or pushing costs outside the budgetary window.

There has to be a better way to do things.

Budget Process Reform Sorely Needed

Created in 1974, the current budget process has been subjected to over 30 years of abuse from lawmakers trying to exploit its structural flaws. Instead of providing an orderly roadmap for determining the nation's annual spending and revenue priorities, the current budget process stifles debate, prevents cooperation, and frequently breaks down.

The flaws in the budget process are numerous. No statutory spending caps exist that require lawmakers to set priorities and make trade-offs. Even modest congressional budget restraints are routinely overridden by a simple majority vote in the House of Representatives and a three-fifths vote in the Senate. When crafting annual budgets, the president and Congress are not brought together to agree on a basic framework until the end of the process. Once the appropriations process begins, two-thirds of the budget is deemed "uncontrollable" and excluded from the oversight of annual appropriations. Emergency spending is also typically excluded from annual appropriations bills and is instead relegated to *ad hoc* [improvised] budgeting outside of normal budget constraints. Static tax scoring and baseline budgeting create biases in favor of spending increases and against tax cuts. Budgeting by credit card, Congress does not even measure its own long-term financial commitments. Overall, the broken budget process has enabled Congress's spending spree and hindered rational allocation of taxpayer dollars.

Brian M. Riedl, "10 Elements of Comprehensive Budget Process Reform," Backgrounder, No. 1943, June 15, 2006. www.heritage.org/research/budget/bg1943.cfm.

Serious and Thoughtful Reform Is Needed

An improved budget should meet a few basic criteria. It has to be simple and realistic enough to set credible limits on spending and tax bills. The budget process should provide incentives for lawmakers to engage openly in the inherent trade-offs of real budgeting. And they should work within a framework that takes the country's entire fiscal picture into account: Entitlements, discretionary spending, and taxes all have to be on the table. And perhaps most importantly, to ensure that we don't make decisions that endanger our country's fiscal health down the road, the budget should give ample consideration to the long-term ramifications of entitlement and tax policies. Finally, a good budget process has to be backed up with tough enforcement mechanisms: Whether through enforceable limits on expenditures, some form of PAYGO [Pay-As-You-GO], or a new mechanism, lawmakers must be held accountable for their budgetary decisions.

To address this critical issue, the Committee for a Responsible Federal Budget, working with the Peterson and Pew foundations, has assembled a bipartisan team of experts for a budget reform commission. This effort is modeled after a noted 1967 budget concept commission that laid the foundation for today's consolidated budget. As our government spends trillions to pull the country back from recession, the crisis in the economy has spilled over into the budget. And once we begin to repair this budgetary damage, we will be hit by a long-term structural imbalance between spending and revenue that requires even harder choices. The need for serious and thoughtful reform has perhaps never been greater.

| "Statutory PAYGO is a small, but important step toward restoring fiscal discipline to the federal budget."

A PAYGO Statute Is an Effective Budgetary Policy

Alice M. Rivlin

Alice M. Rivlin, the founding director of the Congressional Budget Office, is now a senior fellow in economic studies at the Brookings Institution. In the following viewpoint, she explains her support for a pay-as-you-go (PAYGO) statute to the House of Representatives Budget Committee. She believes that enacting PAYGO legislation is a necessary first step toward decreasing the federal budget deficit. The PAYGO rules in place from 1991 through 2002, she says, proved highly effective in deterring deficit-increasing expenditures. Therefore, she says, a PAYGO statute should be imposed again on new spending.

As you read, consider the following questions:

1. What does Rivlin believe may result from the U.S. government's creditors' loss of faith in the American economy?

Alice M. Rivlin, "Statutory PAYGO: An Important First Step Toward Fiscal Responsibility," U.S. House of Representatives, June 18, 2009. Reproduced by permission of the author.

2. According to Rivlin, why were the effects of PAYGO not visible to the public or press in the 1990s?

3. Why does Rivlin believe the four exceptions to the PAYGO law should remain?

Enshrining in law the PAYGO [pay-as-you-go] rules which Congress adopted in 2007 would highlight their importance and make them easier to enforce. Statutory PAYGO is a small, but important step toward restoring fiscal discipline to the federal budget. Along with President [Barack] Obama, the Blue Dog Coalition, and many other proponents of responsible federal budgeting, I urge you to take this step without delay.

No one needs to remind this [House of Representatives Budget] Committee that the outlook for the federal budget is worrisome—indeed, scary. Long before the financial crisis and the current deep recession, this Committee was anxiously pointing out that current federal spending and revenue policies are on a risky, unsustainable course. Promises made under the major entitlement programs (especially Medicare and Medicaid) will increase federal spending rapidly over the next couple of decades, as the population ages and medical spending continues to rise faster than other spending. Federal expenditures are projected to grow substantially faster than revenues, opening widening deficit gaps that cannot not be financed.

The financial crisis and the recession, combined with the measures the government has taken to mitigate both, have worsened the budget outlook dramatically. The federal deficit will probably reach 13 percent of the GDP [gross domestic product] this year [2009] and will likely remain at worrisome levels even as the economy recovers. Federal debt held by the public, including our foreign creditors, is projected to double as a percent of GDP over the next decade. The recent rise in long term Treasury rates is a timely reminder that our creditors, foreign and domestic, may lose faith in America's willingness to take the difficult steps necessary to move the budget toward balance. This loss of faith—reversing the widespread perception that U.S. Treasuries are the safest securities in the world—could lead to rapidly rising interest rates, killer debt service costs for the federal government and others, a plunging dollar, and an aborted recovery.

Immediate Action Is Necessary

As I testified before this Committee on January 27, 2009, I strongly believe that most of the emergency actions that authorities have taken to stimulate the economy and rescue the financial sector were the right policies in these dire circumstances. An escalating deficit and huge amounts of debt were necessary to avoid a much deeper and longer recession and a total meltdown of the financial system. However, these actions have made it absolutely necessary for Congress and the Administration to work together aggressively to bring future deficits under control. Unpopular actions to restrain future spending and augment future revenues must be taken *now*, even before recovery has been achieved. Putting Social Security on a sound fiscal base, credibly reducing the rate of growth of federal health spending, and raising future energy-related and other revenues are all actions that could be taken now to reduce future deficits.

Immediate actions to reduce long-term deficits—such as fixing Social Security this year—will enhance the prospects for recovery by restoring confidence in government and reducing long-term interest rates. These actions to reduce future deficits will require political courage. Stronger budgetary rules, such as statutory PAYGO, can bolster political courage.

Statutory PAYGO: One Tool for Fiscal Discipline

PAYGO is budget speak for "do no harm" or "don't make future deficits worse." PAYGO rules are designed to discourage Congress and the administration from enacting legislation that would add new mandatory benefits or reduce revenues without taking other actions that would have equal and opposite effects on the deficit over a ten-year period. Statutory PAYGO affecting both mandatory spending and taxes was in effect from 1991 through 2002, when the legislation lapsed and was not reenacted. Currently PAYGO is part of the House and Senate rules, but [it] does not have the force of law.

I believe that statutory PAYGO proved a highly effective deterrent to deficit-increasing legislation in the 1990s—at least until the surplus was achieved in 1998. The effects of PAYGO were not visible to the public or the press because they involved spending and taxing proposals that never saw the light of day. At the Office of Management [and Budget] (OMB) in President [Bill] Clinton's first term, my uncomfortable job was to tell the president and the rest of the administration that many of their most cherished ideas could not even be proposed because we could not find a way to offset them under the PAYGO rules. Similar conversations took place in congressional committees. Detractors of PAYGO, who point out that a serious sequestration [automatic spending cut] has never been enforced, miss the point that sequestration is a deterrent, not a policy. It would be a more powerful deterrent if it could be waived only by enacting a law subject to veto. I believe sequestration would be even more effective as a deterrent if there were fewer exceptions to its automatic cuts.

The Difficult Problem of Defining the Baseline

The most difficult decision in designing a strong PAYGO rule is answering the question, "Don't make deficits worse compared to what?" Should the baseline be strictly current law or a more realistic appraisal of what is likely to happen? In general, it is best to stick with current law, because it is the easiest rule to understand and explain. However, occasionally extending currently law is clearly not what most people expect to happen.

PAYGO Is a Necessary First Step

PAYGO will not be a panacea [cure-all], but it will be a necessary first step. Paying-as-you-go requires Congress to make tough choices, but these types of choices are ones that families and households must make every day. It's past time that Congress be held to the same standard. Rhetoric should be mirrored by laws that mandate its execution. I have co-sponsored PAYGO legislation to do just that. . . .

Nicola Tsongas,
"Return of 'PAYGO' Would Reduce Deficit,"
Wicked Local Lancaster, *June 25, 2009.*
www.wickedlocal.com.

President Obama's statutory PAYGO proposal recognizes that four specific provisions of existing law are so unrealistic that incorporating them in a current law baseline would make the PAYGO rule unworkable. The proposal recognizes that Medicare payments to physicians under Part B will not automatically be cut by 21 percent as the law requires; the estate and gift tax will not expire in 2010 and return to pre-2001 levels in 2011; that the current AMT patch [the Alternative Minimum Tax; the patch keeps middle-income taxpayers protected from the AMT, which was intended to guarantee that wealthy taxpayers with many write-offs still paid some amount of tax] will not be allowed to expire without replacement; and that all of the 2001 and 2003 tax provisions will not all expire at the end of 2010. Critics of the Administration's proposal point out that allowing these adjustments to a current law baseline amounts to accepting the damage already done to future budgets that these bizarre legislative provisions were designed to hide. They argue that in making these exceptions

Congress would be ducking the responsibility to face the consequences past lack of budgetary courage. I agree that these are four examples of legislative sleight of hand covering up future bad news. But the bad news must be dealt with head-on in a comprehensive policy process. Keeping these four legislative anomalies in the current law baseline for PAYGO purposes would only guarantee that PAYGO would be immediately waived and its future usefulness seriously impaired.

Moving Beyond Statutory PAYGO

While I support the administration's proposal for statutory PAYGO, I regard it as a small first step on the arduous path that will move the budget to long-run sustainability. We also need firm caps on discretionary spending. But the biggest threat to future budget solvency is not new legislation; it is the budgetary consequences of legislative decisions already made—both with respect to mandatory spending and the tax code.

While the current annual budget process involves Herculean efforts to scrutinize discretionary spending, it leaves entitlement programs and revenues on automatic pilot outside the budget process. Fiscal responsibility requires that all long-term spending commitments be subject to periodic review along with taxes and tax expenditures. There is no compelling logic for applying caps and intense annual scrutiny to discretionary spending, while leaving huge spending commitments, such as Medicare or the home mortgage deduction entirely outside the budget process and not subject to review on a regular basis. Nor is there any good reason for subjecting new mandatory spending and revenue legislation to an elaborate PAYGO procedure while ignoring the budget implications of past legislation.

I am a member of a bipartisan group called the Fiscal Seminar (sponsored by the Brookings Institution and the Heritage Foundation) that addressed this problem [in 2008] in a controversial paper entitled "Taking Back Our Fiscal Future." We proposed that Congress enact long-run budgets for the three biggest entitlement programs. These budgets would be reviewed every five years. Spending overruns would trigger automatic spending cuts or revenue increases that would take effect unless Congress acted. We recognized that we had proposed only a partial solution—the tax side of the budget should be included—and others may have better ideas. However, we clearly identified a glaring defect in the budget process that stands in the way of getting the federal budget on a sustainable long-run track. We believe it is imperative for Congress to adopt a new budget process that includes *all* spending and revenue and subjects the budget impacts of long-term commitments to serious periodic review.

"*PAYGO is merely a distraction from real budget reforms that could rein in runaway spending and budget deficits.*"

A PAYGO Statute Is Bad Budgetary Policy

Brian M. Riedl

Brian M. Riedl is the Grover M. Hermann Fellow in Federal Budgetary Affairs at the Thomas A. Roe Institute for Economic Policy Studies at the Heritage Foundation. In the next viewpoint, he writes that President Barack Obama's PAYGO statute is more of a political gimmick than an effective policy. One problem with PAYGO is that it can be waived—and history has shown that lawmakers frequently take advantage of this capability. Furthermore, those expenditures that take up the greatest portion of the federal budget, such as discretionary spending, are exempt from PAYGO rules. Riedl contends that these loopholes and others render PAYGO futile.

As you read, consider the following questions:

1. According to Riedl, how would a PAYGO statute work differently from a PAYGO rule?

Brian M. Riedl, "Obama's PAYGO Law Would Not Slow Spending or Budget Deficits," Heritage Foundation Web Memo, February 26, 2009. Copyright © 2009 The Heritage Foundation. Reproduced by permission.

2. Why does Riedl disapprove of PAYGO's classification of tax cut extensions as new tax cuts?

3. What accounts for the temporarily balanced budget during the last PAYGO period, according to Riedl?

A week after muscling through possibly the most expensive spending bill in America history, President [Barack] Obama has called on Congress to support fiscal discipline. Specifically, he has proposed a Pay-as-You-Go (PAYGO) statute requiring that tax cuts and entitlement [programs such as Social Security and Medicare] expansions be collectively deficit neutral.

Since 2007, Congress has had a PAYGO rule mandating that each new tax and entitlement bill be deficit neutral. Because it is merely a congressional rule, lawmakers can (and do) waive it easily. By contrast, a PAYGO *statute*—which existed from 1991 until 2002—would operate differently. Instead of requiring that each tax and entitlement bill be deficit neutral, this law would keep a running scorecard of all enacted bills (allowing one bill to offset another). If, at the end of the year, the net effect of all tax and entitlement legislation was to increase the budget deficit over the next decade, an automatic series of entitlement spending cuts ("sequestrations") would be triggered to offset those costs.

PAYGO has proven to be more of a talking point than an actual tool for budget discipline. During the 1991–2002 round of statutory PAYGO, Congress and the president still added more than $700 billion to the budget deficit and simply cancelled every single sequestration. Since the 2007 creation of the PAYGO rule, Congress has waived it numerous times and added $600 billion to the deficit.

Creating a PAYGO law and then blocking its enforcement is inconsistent and hypocritical. And given their recent waiving of PAYGO to pass a $1.1 trillion stimulus bill, there is no reason to believe the current Congress and the president are any more likely to enforce PAYGO than their predecessors were. And even if it were enforced, PAYGO applies to only a small fraction of federal spending (new entitlements). Consequently, PAYGO is merely a distraction from real budget reforms that could rein in runaway spending and budget deficits.

Too Many Exemptions

PAYGO Would Not Decrease the Growth of Federal Spending. PAYGO is not designed to reduce federal spending. It is not even designed to slow the growth rate of spending. It *only* limits the creation of *new* entitlement benefits above the spending growth baseline. In fact, entitlement spending grew *faster* after statutory PAYGO took effect in 1991.

PAYGO Exempts Discretionary Spending. Discretionary spending programs—which comprise nearly 40 percent of the federal budget—are totally exempt from PAYGO rules. In other words, Congress could provide unlimited budget increases to most defense, education, health research, justice, international, environmental, veterans' health, homeland security, and housing programs without triggering PAYGO. This loophole is a major flaw that substantially weakens PAYGO.

PAYGO Exempts Current Entitlement Benefits. Under PAYGO, current entitlement programs can continue to grow on autopilot. Only newly created entitlement benefits must be offset. In short, PAYGO would not prevent:

- Social Security from growing 6 percent annually;

- Medicare and Medicaid from growing 7 percent annually; and

- Nominal entitlement spending from nearly doubling over the next decade.

PAYGO could theoretically slow down the creation of any new entitlements. Yet the nation's main budgetary challenges stem from the $44 trillion unfunded obligation from Social Security and Medicare, as well as the growing costs of current entitlements [such as] Medicaid. PAYGO would do nothing to reduce the growth rate of these programs.

A Double Standard

PAYGO Employs a Double Standard That Raises Taxes. Every few years, Congress must review and renew most entitlement programs and many tax cuts. PAYGO sensibly says that renewing an existing entitlement program is not "new" spending and therefore does not need to be offset. However, PAYGO applies a different standard to tax cuts. It classifies tax cut extensions as "new" tax cuts that violate PAYGO and must be offset.

This makes no sense. PAYGO was intended to block the creation of *new* policies that increase the deficit. Simply keeping current tax policies in place should not be treated as "new" tax cuts. Additionally, the blatant double standard of allowing entitlement spending policies but not tax policies to be extended constitutes a major bias towards higher taxes and spending. For instance, PAYGO allows the extension of expiring SCHIP [State Children's Health Insurance Program] and farm subsidy laws, but it does not allow the extension of the 2001 and 2003 tax cuts or the Alternative Minimum Tax (AMT) to be patched without offsets. Even President Obama has criticized this double standard, and Congress should eliminate this baseline disparity from any PAYGO statute.

Lack of Enforcement

Previous PAYGO Statutes Were Never Enforced—Not Even Once. Congress already had a PAYGO statute from 1991 to 2002. But this law was never enforced. Over the statute's 12 years, Congress enacted more than $700 billion in new entitlement spending and tax cuts—and then enacted legislation cancelling every single sequestration. Even if Congress had allowed sequestration, they had already enacted legislation exempting

The PAYGO Cover-up

As [President Barack] Obama knows but won't tell voters, paygo only applies to *new or expanded* entitlement programs, not to existing programs such as Medicare, this year [2009] growing at a 9.2% annual rate. Nor does paygo apply to discretionary spending, set to hit $1.4 trillion in fiscal 2010, or 40% of the budget.

This loophole matters, because on the very day Mr. Obama was hailing paygo the House Appropriations Committee was gleefully approving a 12% increase in 2010 nondefense discretionary spending.

"The 'Paygo' Coverup,"
The Wall Street Journal, *June 12, 2009.*

97 percent of all entitlement spending—all but $31 billion—from being part of any sequestration. The law was practically designed to fail. Entitlement spending actually grew *faster* during the 12 years of PAYGO (1991–2002) than in the 12 previous years (1980–1991).

The budget did temporarily achieve balance during that period. Yet PAYGO had very little to do with it. The budget was balanced by the combination of the dot com bubble revenue boom, defense savings after the Cold War ended, and declining net interest costs.

Current PAYGO Rules Are Not Enforced. Congress has operated under a PAYGO rule since 2007. In that short period of time, Congress has already bypassed PAYGO to:

- Enact a stimulus bill that costs $479 billion in new entitlements and tax cuts;

- Enact a veterans' education entitlement bill costing $63 billion;

- Enact a student loan expansion costing $15 billion;

- Twice patch the AMT; and

- Enact SCHIP and farm bills that used blatant gimmicks to hide tens of billions of dollars in new entitlement benefits.

Congress has bypassed PAYGO every time it has proved even slightly inconvenient to its spending agenda. There is no reason to believe another PAYGO statute would be any more successful.

Suggested Improvements

Even if PAYGO were miraculously enforced, baseline entitlement cost increases would still push the size of the federal government to nearly 50 percent of [gross domestic product, or GDP] by 2050. PAYGO would also promote the expiration of all 2001 and 2003 tax cuts and force millions of Americans to pay the AMT. As a result, tax revenues would rise from the historical average of 18.3 percent of GDP to a record 23.5 percent by 2050. The slow-growth economies of western Europe show that such levels of spending and taxation cause serious long-term economic damage.

If a statutory PAYGO law is to be enacted, President Obama and Congress should address some of the problems by:

- Making sure PAYGO treats tax and entitlement programs equally. If the renewal of expiring entitlement programs does not trigger PAYGO, neither should the renewal of expiring tax cuts.

- Pledging to block any legislation cancelling a PAYGO sequestration. Otherwise, Congress will continue to expand entitlements without paying for them.

- Avoiding the past practice of exempting 97 percent of entitlement spending from sequestration, which would otherwise render the law ineffective.

- Enacting statutory discretionary spending caps to close the loophole exempting non-entitlement spending.

- Enacting tougher entitlement controls by setting multi-year spending targets for entitlement programs covered by PAYGO. If OMB [Office of Management and Budget] projects that spending will exceed these targets, the President would be required to submit reform proposals to reduce spending as part of the annual budget request, and Congress would have to act on those proposals.

Worse Than Doing Nothing

It is easy to suggest that even an ineffective PAYGO would be no worse than the status quo. This ignores PAYGO's bias for painful tax increases. Also, by providing a false sense of security, PAYGO would slow the momentum for vital budget process reforms that could actually rein in spending and the deficits. At the very least, the president should reduce Congress's ability to game the system by adding the improvements noted above to his PAYGO proposal.

"Supplemental spending, 'emergency' spending in particular, has become Washington's tool of choice for evading annual budget limits and increasing spending across the board."

The Supplemental Appropriations Process Is Currently Being Abused

Veronique de Rugy

In the following viewpoint, Veronique de Rugy, a senior research fellow at the Mercatus Center at George Mason University, discusses Congress's misuse of the supplemental appropriations process. While the process is set up for programs that arise that cannot wait for the next year's budget, Congress has been using it to fund anything that might not be approved through the regular budget process, such as the Iraq War. By funding the war with supplemental appropriations, de Rugy contends that the George W. Bush administration was able to hide the true cost of the war from the American people.

Veronique de Rugy, "The Federal Budget's Long Emergency," *Reason*, December 2006. Copyright © 2006 by Reason Foundation, 3415 S. Sepulveda Blvd., Suite 400, Los Angeles, CA 90034, www.reason.com. Reproduced by permission.

As you read, consider the following questions:

1. By how much did the Republican Congress expand federal spending since fiscal year 2001, according to de Rugy?

2. How do requests for supplemental appropriations money differ from regular budget requests?

3. Who deserves most of the blame for the abuse of the supplemental appropriations process, in de Rugy's view?

Will giving $150 million to the National Oceanic and Atmospheric Administration help win the wars in Iraq and Afghanistan? How about spending $500 million to repair a shipyard and an extra $2.3 billion for avian flu preparedness, on top of the $3.8 billion already appropriated for that purpose? Congress and the White House think so. All those expenditures are part of a $94.5 billion supplemental spending bill for the war on terror and hurricane relief signed by President [George W.] Bush in June [2006].

Politicians may cry crocodile [false] tears about deficit spending, but their actions demonstrate that they remain addicted to big government. The Republican Congress that has expanded federal spending by 45 percent since fiscal year 2001, more than doubled education spending, and enacted insanely expensive agriculture, highway, energy, and prescription drug bills is still bingeing on our tax dollars. But instead of working through the regular appropriations process, Congress is hiding behind "emergency" supplemental bills.

Supplemental spending, "emergency" spending in particular, has become Washington's tool of choice for evading annual budget limits and increasing spending across the board. Funding predictable, nonemergency needs through supplementals hides skyrocketing military costs and allows Congress to boost regular appropriations for both defense and nondefense programs, thereby enabling the spending explosion of the last five years.

War-by-Supplemental Must Stop

A growing number of lawmakers—Republicans as well as Democrats—are raising objections to war-by-supplemental. "Last year, we were pretty clear, on both sides of the aisle, in this and the other body, that we think supplemental funding needs to stop," said Rep. Ike Skelton, D-Mo., the ranking member on the House Armed Services Committee, at a February hearing on the defense budget. "Congress and the American people must be able to see the full cost of the war, and it must be done through the regular process, not through supplementals."

David Baumann, "War, Off the Books,"
National Journal, *April 22, 2006.*

A Good Idea, in Theory

In theory, supplemental appropriations provide additional funding to an agency during the course of a fiscal year for programs and activities that are considered too urgent to wait until the next year's budget. The Budget Enforcement Act of 1990 gives emergency bills special exemptions from rules designed to restrain spending. For instance, the requests lack the level of detail used to justify the federal government's annual budget requests, making accountability more difficult, and supplemental funding is left out of the deficit projections that accompany the annual budget.

Although there are no limits on the amount or type of spending that can be designated an emergency requirement, historically there [had] been an understanding that emergencies are sudden, urgent, unforeseen, and temporary conditions that pose a threat to life, property, or national security. Not

How Effective Is the Current Federal Budget Process?

anymore. For years, Congress has abused its emergency spending powers. But things have gotten much worse since Republicans won control at both ends of Pennsylvania Avenue [over the legislative and executive branches of the federal government].

Supplemental Spending Has Risen Dramatically

Except for a sharp spike in 1991 to fund the first Gulf War, supplemental appropriations remained at roughly 1 percent of new discretionary spending during most of the 1990s. After 1998, they started to rise as the federal budget began running surpluses. But in those days, the United States still enjoyed the benefits of a divided [between Republican and Democrat control] government. After 2002 Republicans conveniently allowed the few budget rules meant to constrain their behavior to expire. Hence supplemental appropriations designated as emergency spending no longer count against the annual budget limits set by Congress and do not trigger automatic cuts if they push outlays above the caps. In fiscal year 2005, supplemental appropriations represented 16.7 percent of new discretionary spending and, adjusted for inflation, reached an all time high of $143 billion—up from $7 billion in fiscal year 1998, when supplementals accounted for 0.9 percent of new discretionary spending. And this year's $94.5 billion supplemental bill is the largest one ever.

The White House deserves most of the blame. The Bush administration has used supplementals to hide the true cost of the wars in Iraq and Afghanistan. Three years in, the Iraq war can hardly be called an emergency or an unpredictable event. This is especially true since one of the largest expenditures goes to the salaries and benefits of Army National Guard personnel and reservists called to active duty. Yet each year President Bush leaves out all war costs when he presents his budget to Congress, knowing that he will be able to secure the fund-

43

ing later through the supplemental process. This year Congress will appropriate nearly 20 percent of total military spending via supplementals.

Deceitful Spending

Meanwhile, the lack of detail in supplemental budget requests and their expedited approval process have made supplemental bills a magnet for pork and other projects that wouldn't be funded on their own merits. No politician wants to vote against emergency aid money aimed at supporting U.S. troops in Iraq or helping victims of Hurricane Katrina. And because the president—especially this president—. . . usually [signs] emergency bills without blinking at their cost, many wasteful nonemergency spending items go through at taxpayers' expense.

This year's emergency spending bill, for instance, contains $118 million to bail out private fisheries, on top of tens of billions in disaster relief funds the Federal Emergency Management Agency and the Small Business Administration are already paying to that industry. It also includes $335 million to subsidize "volunteer" work through AmeriCorps [a network of national service programs that engages Americans in volunteer service] and a $703 million add-on for highway projects unrelated to the Gulf Coast—some of them in Hawaii and California. Those aren't the only projects in the bill that aren't anywhere near Iraq or the Gulf Coast: There are Army Corps of Engineers earmarks for North Padre Island, Texas; Sacramento, California; and water systems across Hawaii.

Expect more bills like this in the future. Waste is endemic in Congress, and the White House has refused to restrain the legislature's spending explosion. Until that changes, politicians will still claim with straight faces that $500 million for farm and ranch subsidies or $500,000 for the Mississippi Children's Museum qualify as "emergency" spending.

| "The time for an earmark moratorium
has arrived."

Earmarks Are Bad Budgetary Policy

Mike Pence

In the following viewpoint, Representative Mike Pence of Indiana argues that the current congressional system of earmarking must be stopped and then fundamentally reformed. Earmarking allows spending requests to be approved without meaningful scrutiny, resulting in numerous unnecessary projects funded with large chunks of budgetary money. Many earmarks have been approved through outright corrupt practices. If earmarks are to stay, Pence argues, they must be used with more openness and care. Until then, a moratorium should be imposed on the practice of earmarking.

As you read, consider the following questions:

1. What political shift in 2006 was partially caused by public concern over spending, according to Pence?

2. What was the total cost of the earmarks passed in 2007?

Mike Pence, "Earmarking Reform," *Washington Times*, February 5, 2008, Op-Ed. Copyright © 2008 Washington Times LLC. Reproduced by permission.

3. According to Pence, what "significant step toward earmark reform" was taken by Congressional Republicans after losing control of the House?

Airplane pilots know that when you're flying a plane and the gauges start telling you something is wrong, the first thing you do is put the airplane on the ground, check out the engine and figure out what's wrong.

After years of excess spending and outright corruption, the gauges of federal spending in Washington are telling the American people something is very wrong, especially when it comes to earmarks. It is time to land the plane and fix the engine. It is time for an earmark moratorium followed by fundamental reform.

Earmarking occurs when a member of Congress requests funding for specific projects in their districts and states. Such spending is as old as the republic itself. Under the Constitution, Congress has the authority to spend the people's money in ways both large and small. I have requested earmarked spending every year that I have been in office.

However, directing spending in the form of earmarks must be done wisely, openly and fairly. Earmarking in recent years has not met the high standard the American people demand. The federal budget system, including earmarking, is broken. Earmarking came of age under Republican control of Congress with thousands of projects being added to bills that had never included such spending. Public concern over spending was a major factor in the defeat of the Republican majority in 2006.

Democrats Did Not Fulfill Promise of Reform

Despite promises of reform from Democrats when they won the congressional majority, earmarking continues to spiral out of control. Last year's [2007] omnibus spending bill was more

"HOLD IT RIGHT THERE, CONGRESSMAN! YOU DIDN'T SIGN IN."

than 3,400 pages long, and it wasn't filed until after midnight on the very day the vote was held. Members did not have time to review it. If they had, they would have found that it contained wasteful earmark spending ranging from funding fruit fly research to building swimming pools to providing for wine and culinary centers. Most egregious, they would have found that nearly 300 unexamined earmarks costing more than $800 million were dropped in at the last minute, in the middle of the night, immune to public debate or scrutiny until after the fact.

[Spending] bills passed in 2007 included some 11,000 earmarks. Those earmarks totaled more than $14 billion in cost and included wasteful spending for items such as a $20 million ferry in Alaska to connect Anchorage with Port MacKenzie—benefiting just 40 people who work in Port MacKenzie. That, of course, followed the infamous Bridge to Nowhere earmark from the 2005 highway bill. The current system of earmarking allows this waste to continue. It allows earmarks to be requested for projects hundreds of miles away from the districts that the requesting member represents, and it has led to earmarks being tied to public scandals and outright corruption.

House Republicans Calling for a "Time-Out"

I have been an advocate for earmark reform for years and have led efforts by House conservatives to enact budget process reforms under Republican majorities. I have also supported bipartisan efforts to enact further earmark reforms under Democratic control. And I have led by example. I have never traded my vote for a funding request. One year ago [2007], my office was among the first in Congress to post all of my appropriations requests on my Web site. I have made every effort to press for reform within the system, but I have come to the conclusion that Congress must take dramatic action to restore public confidence in the federal budget process.

After seeing House Democrats return to "earmarks as usual," including hundreds of unexamined earmarks in recent spending bills, I believe that the time for an earmark moratorium has arrived. And House Republicans have risen to the challenge. Recently, Republicans in Congress took a significant step toward earmark reform by challenging House Democrats to join them in a "time-out" on earmarking. Republicans united behind a challenge for an earmark moratorium and called for the establishment of a new select committee that would conduct public hearings and make recommendations that will change the way that Congress spends the people's money. .... By challenging House Democrats to join in a bipartisan effort ending the current practice of earmarking in Washington, House Republicans have thrown down the gauntlet of reform.

Americans Want Earmark Reform

Should Democrats refuse this bipartisan challenge, choosing to defend the current system for earmark spending, they will have dismissed the heartfelt concern of millions of Americans who long to see integrity restored in the national legislature. If Democrats refuse to join us in the cause of reform, Republicans will continue to press for an earmark moratorium and fundamental reform. Nothing short of a full moratorium followed by a public vetting of the current system will restore public confidence in our federal budget.

America wants Congress to land the plane, embrace a moratorium on earmarks and fix this broken system. Republicans are leading this fight for fiscal discipline and reform. For the sake of the nation, I sincerely hope our Democrat colleagues will soon follow.

> *"Obviously earmarks should be transparent; obviously they can be wasteful and the process can be deformed; but earmarks can also be justified and even essential."*

Earmarks Are Effective Budgetary Policy

Robert Shrum

In this viewpoint, Robert Shrum argues that Republicans such as Senator John McCain place too much weight on the negative economic impact of earmarks. Republicans offer examples of wasteful earmark spending, but many cited programs are quite valuable. Furthermore, there is plenty of wasteful spending outside of earmarks. The current economic crisis, he says, requires a much bigger solution than eliminating earmarks. Republicans' attacks on earmarks are primarily just a means to attack Democratic economic policies. Robert Shrum was an adviser to the 2000 Gore and 2004 Kerry presidential campaigns and is the author of No Excuses: Confessions of a Serial Campaigner.

As you read, consider the following questions:

1. According to Shrum, why did President Barack Obama refuse to veto the holdover appropriations bill?

2. How might the "promotion of astronomy" in Hawaii help the economy, in Shrum's view?

3. Why did John McCain lose the 2008 presidential election, according to Shrum?

Last week [March 1–7, 2009], the beleaguered Republicans in Congress finally moved on from attempting to inflict collateral damage on President [Barack] Obama by ritually scourging "[Harry] Reid and [Nancy] Pelosi." They explicitly blamed the president for his willingness to sign a holdover appropriations bill supposedly replete with "earmarks"—a word which has now become the equivalent of a budgetary profanity. Senate minority leader Mitch McConnell was too earmarked up himself to lead the charge, although he did organize behind the lines to temporarily deny the Democrats the needed sixty votes to move ahead in the Senate.

The claimed goal here was to pressure the president to threaten a veto—over earmarks that constitute about 1% of the 410-billion-dollar measure—a political tactic to expose him as a hypocrite for failing to do so since he was critical of earmarks during the campaign. His criticism, however, is more muted than John McCain's; the latter often left the impression that his entire answer to the economic crisis was eliminating earmarks like the now iconic "Bridge to Nowhere."

Obama, of course, declined to rise to the Republican bait. For one thing, as administration officials rightly noted, the bill is last year's business, a holdover from the final dreary and deadlocked denouement of the [George W.] Bush administration. . . . A veto would gum up the legislative gears, requiring a time-consuming new effort to deal with old issues and stirring resentments that could cost the President vital support for his budget. This was never in the cards, but was the ultimate Republican aim—to slow or derail the Obama economic program.

McCain's Examples Fail to Prove His Point

In the midst of the greatest economic crisis since the 1930s, who other than the angry, self-righteous John McCain would pause or detour to do mortal combat with earmarks? Yet most of the press echoed the Republican line, even the *New York Times*, which reported the probably weeklong delay in passing the bill as a Democratic "failure" and then offered up a name brand Op-Ed column that uncritically reprinted McCain's manic twitterings.

The story line is probably just too easy, the punch lines too irresistible. During the stimulus debate, we had a run of stories across the media about Obama's stumbles and setbacks—just before the largest single expenditure bill in American history passed in record time and the president's approval rating reached [historical] highs. But it's even easier to go down the high-minded road here, because the examples McCain cites are the very caricature of a hapless, spendthrift Congress.

Never mind that many of the most glaring items could in fact help the economy. New York's wine industry will benefit from research in grape genetics. "Quick, peel me a grape," McCain twittered, ignoring the potential boost for production and jobs. The same goes for the "earmark" for blueberry farming in Georgia, catfish research in Alabama, and the "promotion of astronomy" in Hawaii. The luddite McCain noted that "nothing says jobs for average Americans like investing in astronomy." Well, yes it does—if they're hired to build the equipment or staff the facilities. The most egregious McCain reach for the cheap and the demagogic was his cute denunciation of a million dollar appropriation for "Mormon cricket control in Utah," which he ridiculed as possibly "a game played by the

Today's Earmarking System Makes Sense

Political discretion can be abused, and one would certainly not want most federal spending to be subject to it. But, provided that transparency is assured, shouldn't there be a place in government for elected officials to exercise judgment in the use of taxpayer money? In fact, if you wanted to create a nonbureaucratic, transparent system of rapid-response grants for pressing local concerns, you would come up with something very much like today's earmarking system (and you'd call it "reinventing government").

Some earmark spending is silly, but then so is some non-earmark spending and there is a lot more of the latter.

Jonathan Rauch,
"Earmarks Are a Model, Not a Menace,"
National Journal, *March 14, 2009.*

brits." (In twitter-land, presumably there are no capital letters.) Clearly, McCain hasn't even glanced at the issue. It has nothing to do with the British, or with "Mormon crickets" who adjure alcohol and coffee; it's about pests who endanger crops, livelihoods, and yes, guess again, agriculture that contributes to economic growth.

Many Earmarks Are Essential

My plight is not that all earmarks are right, but that they're like all forms of government spending. They have to be evaluated on the merits, not libeled by labeling. And in an era when more and more power has been seized by the Executive branch, why should we assume that bureaucrats, the usual Republican targets, are uniformly wiser about how to allocate federal dollars than elected members of Congress. There is no underlying philosophy of government here other than opportunistic posturing. Obviously earmarks should be transparent; obviously they can be wasteful and the process can be deformed; but earmarks can also be justified and even essential.

The Iraq Study Group, which led to a fundamental reexamination of conduct of the war, was created with an earmark offered by one congressman, a Republican, who had had enough of Donald Rumsfeld's stubborn insistence that failure was really success. Newt Gingrich's earmark for additional cargo planes in the early 1990s, spending not requested by the Pentagon, provided needed capacity to resupply our forces in Afghanistan.

An equally persuasive case can be made for some of the biggest domestic earmarks like rail transportation projects in New York and Arizona—which total 600 million dollars in the appropriations measure being carpet-bombed by McCain. The new Labor Secretary, Hilda Solis, has been called out for earmarks in the bill that she inserted as a member of Congress. What are they for? Police equipment in some of the hardest pressed neighborhoods of southern California. What's wrong with that?

There Are Larger Issues Than Earmarks

The unexamined earmark is not worth denouncing or discarding. The fault here is not all McCain's or the Republicans'; Evan Bayh, the perennially cliché-hobbled Democratic Senator from Indiana, joined in last week. He insisted that "spending should be held in check before taxes are raised, even on the wealthy"—a sentiment which surely pleased the *Wall Street Journal*, where he was writing. But he conveniently overlooked the reality that all the earmarks in the bill could be eliminated and total spending would barely change.

John McCain campaigned on his enmity toward earmarks. He lost because the country faced far bigger issues. It still does. The present and passing debate—over a contested appropriations bill that will soon reach the President's desk—is merely another way station in the Republicans' wandering search for an idea beyond reflexive opposition—for a coherent alternative to the Obama economic policy. It won't come from House minority leader John Boehner's latest folly, a proposed federal spending freeze which would drive the economy into an accelerating downturn. And it won't come from the gathering conservative argument that the trick here will be to restore the confidence of the Masters of the Market who, with the connivance of the regulators who didn't, got us into this mess in the first place. This focus on "confidence" was the heart of Herbert Hoover's failed response to the Depression. So, absent any coherent rationale for policy, expect the Republicans to just keep on keeping on. They will relentlessly rationalize a do-nothing, try-everything approach even if it means they have to go along with party-suspect John McCain and for the moment block the earmarks they themselves sponsored.

Periodical Bibliography

The following articles have been selected to supplement the diverse views presented in this chapter.

Edmund L. Andrews	"Emergency Spending as a Way of Life," *New York Times*, October 2, 2005.
David Baumann	"Tempest in a Barrel," *National Journal*, February 11, 2006.
David Baumann	"What, Pork Isn't Kosher?" *National Journal*, February 25, 2006.
Gail Russell Chaddock	"Pesky Earmarks Still in Eye of Budget Storm," *Christian Science Monitor*, March 4, 2009.
Thomas R. Eddlem	"Obama's 'Pay As You Go' Deception," *New American*, June 15, 2009.
Stephen J. Entin	"The Secret Recipe for High Taxes," *Wall Street Journal*, March 14, 2007.
Scot M. Faulkner	"Building a Better Budget," *Washington Times*, February 6, 2007.
Yuval Levin and James C. Capretta	"To Be Continued," *Weekly Standard*, February 26, 2007.
Steven Rattner	"Fudging the Budget," *New York Times*, February 6, 2007.
Ken Silverstein	"The Great American Pork Barrel," *Harper's*, July 2005.
Stephen Spruiell	"Pork Busters, and Keepers," *National Review*, May 8, 2006.
Sheryl Gay Stolberg	"What's Wrong with a Healthy Helping of Pork?" *New York Times*, May 28, 2006.
John Tamny	"Say No to Paygo," *Forbes*, July 6, 2009.
Wall Street Journal	"The 'Paygo' Coverup," June 12, 2009.

OPPOSING
VIEWPOINTS®
SERIES

Cʜᴀᴘᴛᴇʀ 2

How Do Federal Budget Deficits Affect the Nation's Economy?

Chapter Preface

A president's legacy tends to belie the complexity of the times during which he presides. Most Americans tend to associate past presidents with one or two famous accomplishments. For instance, Franklin Delano Roosevelt is associated with the New Deal, Abraham Lincoln is associated with ending slavery, and so on. While all presidents' legacies tend to become simplified as the years pass, the state in which they've left the federal budget is one of the top factors in judgments of past presidents. This is especially true for presidents who have left behind significant budget deficits, or the rare budget surplus.

For instance, President Bill Clinton came into office in 1992 facing a $290 billion budget deficit. In fiscal year 2000, that deficit had turned into a budget surplus of $230 billion, the largest in U.S. history. Despite Clinton's public scandals during his tenure in the Oval Office, including being one of only two U.S. presidents in history to be impeached, he was still number 15 in a 2009 C-SPAN ranking of the best U.S. presidents, based on a poll of 65 historians. In a January 2001 BBC Online article, Steve Schifferes writes, "Mr. Clinton's most enduring legacy is likely to be the economic boom which began shortly before he took office in 1992."

The most recent former president, George W. Bush, has been criticized—and praised—on many accounts, but one of the primary criticisms of him is what he did with the budget surplus he inherited from President Clinton. In a 2005 *New York Times* column, Paul Krugman writes: "President Bush has presided over the transformation of a budget surplus into a large deficit, which threatens the government's long-run solvency. The principal cause of that reversal was Mr. Bush's unprecedented decision to cut taxes, especially on the wealthiest

Americans, while taking the nation into an expensive war." In a 2007 editorial, *USA Today* agrees:

> The government shouldn't be running any deficit on the eve of the baby boomers' retirement. Soaring medical costs, combined with the retirement avalanche, spells massive borrowing and trouble for the economy in coming years.
>
> For not addressing these problems—for, in fact, compounding them with tax cuts and spending increases—Bush deserves blame.

While some pundits add that President Bush inherited a host of problems—particularly, in foreign policy—that needed addressing, many agree that the scale of his spending—particularly on tax cuts—was fiscally irresponsible.

In March 2008, the results of a poll of 109 historians conducted by History News Network were released: 61 percent of them ranked George W. Bush as "worst ever" among U.S. presidents. A flurry of articles has been written, also judging George W. Bush as the worst U.S. president in history. Nearly all of these articles cite Bush's budget deficit as a major factor in this ranking. In a 2006 article called "The Worst President in History?" in *Rolling Stone*, Sean Wilentz writes:

> While wiping out the solid Clinton-era federal surplus and raising federal deficits to staggering record levels, Bush's tax policies have necessitated hikes in federal fees, state and local taxes, and co-payment charges to needy veterans and families who rely on Medicaid, along with cuts in loan programs to small businesses and college students, and in a wide range of state services.

What legacy—economic and otherwise—the current U.S. president, Barack Obama, will leave behind, is unclear at this point. While he has already been criticized for too much spending on economic stimulus packages and bailouts for financial institutions, many pundits have been quick to grant

President Obama some leeway, given the financial crisis he inherited. Given any set of political and economic circumstances, it must also be acknowledged that the president does not have sole control, or responsibility, over the federal budget. As Robert J. Samuelson writes in a 2002 *Washington Post* article, "What presidents and government can't do is guide the economy along a path of trouble-free prosperity. The job is too large; the pressures on the economy are too many; the government's tools (taxes, spending programs, interest rates, regulations) are too few." More important than who deserves blame (or credit) for budget deficits and surpluses is how they affect the country. Exactly how they affect it, the significance of these effects, and what should be done about them, are debated by the authors in the chapter to follow.

> *"There is a tie between budget deficits today and what society can enjoy tomorrow. Eliminating the deficit is an important first step."*

Federal Budget Deficits Are Harmful to the Nation's Economy

Concord Coalition

The Concord Coalition is a nonpartisan organization advocating responsible fiscal policy. In this viewpoint, coalition writers explain the long-term repercussions of budget deficits. They argue that if the current generation leaves a budget deficit behind, future generations will lack sufficient revenue to maintain a prosperous society. Inflation will be more likely, dependence on foreign investors will increase, and the nation will be less equipped for emergencies. Eliminating the deficit is not the only step required for fiscal responsibility, but it is an essential first step toward it.

As you read, consider the following questions:

1. According to the authors, what is the principal way Americans can increase their standard of living?

2. Where does the U.S. government borrow most of its money?

3. Why would a budget deficit increase the likelihood of inflation, according to the authors?

Fiscal responsibility is essential to creating a better, stronger, more prosperous nation for the next generation. The choices we make today—or fail to make—will determine what kind of future our children and grandchildren inherit 20 and 40 years from now.

The nation's economic future and fiscal responsibility are directly linked. There is a tie between budget deficits today and what society can enjoy tomorrow. Eliminating the deficit is an important first step. The larger challenge, however, is to reform our age-related entitlement programs [such as Social Security and Medicare], which are projected to grow at an unsustainable rate as the population ages. Facing up to both the short[-term] and long-term fiscal challenges will help put the nation on a path to lasting prosperity and a rising standard of living. If, on the other hand, we fail to quickly address the growing imbalance between federal commitments and available revenues, we will squander the only opportunity to get our finances in order before the aging of America makes our fiscal situation far more difficult. Doing so would be to ignore every principle of public finance, generational equity, and long-term economic stewardship.

Deficits matter.

Federal Reserve Board Governor Edward M. Gramlich explained the connection between deficits and the future economy at a Concord Coalition policy forum in June 2004:

Fiscal policy can have important long-run effects on the health of the economy, particularly through its impact on national saving and the growth of productivity. National savings can be generated privately, by households and busi-

Sustained Deficits Undermine the Economy

Virtually all mainstream economists agree that, over time, sustained deficits crowd out private investment, increase interest rates, and reduce productivity and economic growth. But, far more dangerously, if markets here and abroad begin to fear long-term fiscal disarray and our related trade imbalances, those markets could then demand sharply higher interest rates for providing long-term debt capital and could put abrupt and sharp downward pressure on the dollar. These market effects, plus the adverse impact of continuing fiscal imbalances on business and consumer confidence, could seriously undermine our economy.

Robert E. Rubin, "Attention: Deficit Disorder,"
New York Times, *May 13, 2005.*

ness, or publicly, by government. Although fiscal policy can, in theory, help boost private saving, this has proven difficult, in practice. Instead, the most important effect of fiscal policy on national saving has been through the direct government budget. When the government runs deficits, it siphons off private savings (reducing national saving), leaving less available for capital investment. With less capital investment, less new equipment is provided to workers, and, all else being equal, future productivity growth rates and levels are lower.

Government Must Have a Pool of Savings

Because there are only so many hours in each day, the principal way Americans can increase their standard of living is if each worker becomes more productive: produces more and better goods and services for each hour worked. This phenomenon is especially important when labor force growth slows—as we expect to happen because of demographic changes in our society, like the aging of the baby boom generation and declining birthrates.

For workers to become more productive, investments must be made in education and training; in modernized plants, equipment, and productive techniques; in new discoveries and innovations; and in transportation, communications, and other infrastructure.

To make these investments, there must be a pool of savings that can be used for this purpose. Historically, the United States has had a particularly low rate of private savings, but, what is worse, the federal government's deficit is financed by soaking up much of the savings we do manage to put away. When the government spends more money than it has, it borrows the rest. Most of the money borrowed comes from private savings.

If deficits are financed by borrowing from domestic lenders, the economy will have less money available for investing here at home in the building blocks of our economic future. If they are financed by foreigners, we will owe a mushrooming debt to the rest of the world, with growing interest costs that must be serviced every year.

As Fed Governor Gramlich summed up in his 2004 Concord Coalition speech,

> Productivity growth is the principal source of improvement in economic well-being. The faster productivity increases over time, the more rapidly living standards increase. Maintaining a rapid rate of trend productivity growth is particularly important in light of the coming budgetary pressures associated with the retirement of the baby boom generation. A more productive economy will ease the financing of Social Security and Medicare benefits for tomorrow's retirees without placing an undue burden on tomorrow's workers. In contrast, if we allow debt to build now and in coming

years, we will have both lower output to meet future obligations as well as the added burden of financing a growing amount of debt. Indeed, under numerous scenarios, our current debt path is unsustainable: Without changes to taxes or spending, we may reach a point where ever-larger amounts of debt must be issued to pay ever-larger interest charges.

To be sure, budget deficits are not always inappropriate, and to a certain extent, the recent fiscal deficits have helped limit the recent economic slowdown. But now that the recovery is well under way, it is important to concentrate on longer-run fiscal policy. Specifically, it is time to bring the budget deficits under control.

Solving the deficit problem does not automatically guarantee a rosy economic future. Other developments are needed to complement a balanced budget: reduced consumption, increasing savings and investment, continued improvements in productivity, improved education, inflation and interest rates at desirable levels, and a favorable worldwide economic climate. But unless we get our deficit problem behind us, we will remain unable to take advantage of these other necessary economic ingredients.

Deficits Diminish Economic Opportunity

We cannot ignore the consequences of deficits much longer. Growing commitments made by one generation to the next cannot be honored on empty pocketbooks. A stagnant long-term economy cannot support retirement payments, medical care, and all the other benefits and services we would like. And it cannot support economic opportunity for today's youth to live as well as their parents' generation.

Massive federal budget deficits threaten our economy in other ways as well. They increase the likelihood of re-igniting inflation by putting pressure on the government simply to print more money to pay off its debt. The more dollars are printed, the less each dollar in your wallet is worth.

As foreign ownership of our resources has grown, so has our dependence on the actions of foreign investors and governments. These entities have come to own more and more of our productive capacity. In addition, foreign investors have bought up over 40 percent of our government's debt held by the public. As foreign holding of U.S. debt grows, so will U.S. interest payments to foreign nationals.

Huge, continual deficits strangle the ability of even a nation as rich as ours to respond when emergencies arise or when new opportunities or problems emerge, including recession. With our government deep in debt and continuing to run huge deficits, we may find it impossible to shoulder new responsibilities.

Ultimately, the choice rests with us. We can demand that our leaders undertake the kinds of reforms, including long-term entitlement reforms, that are needed to put the budget on a sustainable trajectory—and face up to the required sacrifice. Or we can continue to pretend that our choices have no consequences—and let our children pay the price in lost opportunities, lower living standards, and a less safe and secure place in the world.

> *"Neither actual nor projected budget deficits raise real or nominal interest rates, steepen the yield curve, reduce national savings, cause trade deficits or make the dollar go down or up."*

Budget Deficits Are Not as Harmful to the Economy as Many Claim

Alan Reynolds

In the viewpoint below, Cato Institute senior fellow Alan Reynolds writes that the argument that budget deficits result in higher interest rates, diminished economic growth, and increased trade deficits is not backed up by empirical evidence. Furthermore, he states, raising taxes in order to fix the deficit will cause other economic problems, without actually solving the problem. Deficits are caused by too much public spending on entitlement programs such as Social Security and Medicare.

As you read, consider the following questions:

1. According to Reynolds, how do economists treat increases in distortive taxation?

Alan Reynolds, "The Deficit Myths," *Financial Post*, July 7, 2004, p. FP15. Copyright © 2004 Creators Syndicate. All rights reserved. Reproduced by permission of the author.

2. What is the result of increases in taxes, according to the study by Alesina, Ardagna, Perotti, and Schiantarelli?

3. What does Reynolds refer to as the "ageing crisis"?

The U.S. government's swing from budget surpluses to budget deficits has raised concerns about possible negative economic effects. Some economists have argued that deficits will raise interest rates, reduce economic growth, increase trade deficits and possibly create a financial crisis.

A recent study by former Treasury secretary Robert Rubin, Brookings Institution scholar Peter Orszag and economist Allen Sinai argued that projected future deficits affect current interest rates. They also said, among other things, that budget deficits cause trade deficits and that budget deficits cause fiscal disarray and require tax increases to maintain confidence.

Empirical evidence does not support these claims. In reality, neither actual nor projected budget deficits raise real or nominal interest rates, steepen the yield curve [a comparison of interest rates for both short- and long-term bonds], reduce national savings, cause trade deficits or make the dollar go down or up. The logic behind such speculations is flawed and the evidence is missing.

These issues are important because numerous pundits and policy-makers are arguing that taxes should be raised to reduce deficits. Indeed, a theme of Rubin, Orszag and Sinai is that higher tax rates can improve economic growth, a proposition that runs directly counter to serious research on the causes of economic growth. Research on economic growth assigns importance to the tax structure, marginal tax rates and the level and composition of government spending, but not to whether spending is financed by taxes or deficits.

Deficits are a sign that federal spending is too high, but deficits do not cause many of the economic harms that some analysts are claiming.

No Clear Correlation Found

Some economists believe that deficits financed by borrowing increase the demand for capital. This in turn increases the price of capital—i.e., interest rates. Higher interest rates then increase the cost of doing business, which slows down the economy.

Others disagree. In 1987, . . . Robert Barro wrote in his textbook *Macroeconomics* that "this belief does not have evidence to support it." When deficits get bigger, he argued, individuals increase their savings to offset government spending.

Even without assuming Barro's private savings offset, scholars haven't been able to find a clear correlation between interest rates and deficit spending.

Veronique de Rugy,
"When Do Deficits Matter?" Reason, May 2009.

Studies Show Reduction in Spending Leads to Stabilization

The central theme of Rubin, Orszag and Sinai—that higher tax rates can improve growth by raising saving and investment—might be "conventional" at the International Monetary Fund or in some elementary textbooks, but it is quite unconventional when it comes to serious research on the causes of economic growth. Such research assigns importance to marginal tax rates and the structure of taxation and to the level and composition of government spending—but not to whether spending is financed by taxes or debt.

Cross-country empirical studies, such as *Economic Growth* by Robert Barro and Xavier Sala-i-Martin and the *Global Competitiveness Report* from the World Economic Forum, find no significance of budget deficits per se. Economists looking at the sources of economic growth do not treat tax and spending policy as two equally viable devices for changing budget deficits. They treat increases in distortive taxation as a negative influence on economic growth and reduction in government purchases and transfers as a positive influence.

Consider a recent study of 18 countries by Alberto Alesina of Harvard University, Silvia Ardagna of Wellesley College, Robert Perotti of the European University Institute and Fabio Schiantarelli of Boston College. They conclude the following: "First, increases in public spending increase labour costs and reduce profits. As a result, investment declines as well. Second, increases in taxes reduce profits and investment." Above all, they say, fiscal stabilizations that have led to an increase in growth consist mainly of spending cuts, particularly in government wages and transfers, while those associated with a downturn in the economy are characterized by tax increases.

Increasing Taxes Causes Further Economic Harm

The old myth that growth depends on balanced budgets is nowhere to be found in the recent 248-page OECD [Organization for Economic Cooperation and Development] study, *The Sources of Economic Growth in OECD Countries*. The marketing blurb for that study notes: "Growth patterns through the 1990s and into this decade have turned received wisdom on its head ... with the United States notably drawing further ahead of the field."

The OECD's chief economist, Ignazio Visco, writes that "one of the most important lessons to emerge from this work is that ... excessive tax burdens distort proper resource allocation." In particular, the OECD study goes on, "high personal income tax rates can discourage entrepreneurship."

Such microeconomic effects of tax and spending policy can be seriously misunderstood by placing undue emphasis on the gap between planned or realized tax receipts and expenditures, that is, estimated or actual budget deficits.

Government purchases of real resources reduce the availability of labour, equipment and real property, and raise their costs to private businesses. That is why countries that cut government spending, such as Ireland, have had much faster economic growth than countries that pursued costly public works schemes, such as Japan. This "crowding out" is real, not financial. It cannot be reduced by funding government consumption with taxes rather than borrowing.

Government transfer payments are generally given only on the condition that recipients do not work too much, save too much or plant too many crops. If productive effort or saving is even allowed by recipients of transfer payments, the payments are typically reduced or taxed at a higher rate, as in the case of U.S. Social Security. Such programs are a disincentive for those who receive them and also for taxpayers who fund them. These disincentive effects are not reduced by funding transfers with taxes rather than borrowing.

Deficits Are Not the Problem

Demographic projections imply that unfunded promises of Social Security pensions and health care benefits could impose such a heavy tax burden on younger workers in the future that their incentives to work, attend college and save for their own retirement will be severely impaired. This threat of demoralizingly high tax rates on workers and savers is the essence of the "ageing crisis." But converting that threat into a reality by speeding up the taxation of workers cannot solve this problem.

The Congressional Budget Office projects individual tax receipts rising to about 15% of GDP [gross domestic product] by the year 2050, up from about 8% today [2004]. There is nothing in U.S. experience to suggest it would be remotely feasible to double the share of GDP collected by taxes on individual incomes. Looking ahead, it is not future deficits that are unsustainable, it is future transfer payments from unreformed entitlement programs.

Rubin, Orszag, and Sinai have offered hypotheses that purport to predict the effects of estimated future budget deficits on yield curves, real interest rates, national savings, the current account deficit and investor confidence. In reality, neither actual nor projected budget deficits raise real or nominal interest rates, steepen the yield curve, reduce national savings, cause "twin deficits" or make the dollar go down or up. The logic behind such speculations is flawed and contradictory, and the evidence is nonexistent.

> *"Rubinomics, which makes the budget deficit the central focus of economic policy . . . rests on faulty economics."*

The Federal Budget Deficit Should Not Be the Central Focus of U.S. Economic Policy

Thomas Palley

In the following viewpoint, Thomas Palley argues against Rubinomics, the economic philosophy of former Treasury secretary Robert Rubin, which focuses economic policy on eliminating the budget deficit. He disputes the belief that deficits increase interest rates and cause trade deficits. Instead of centering solely on the deficit, Palley says, economic policy should focus on increasing investment, which will result in more jobs and economic growth. Palley is the author of Plenty of Nothing: The Downsizing of the American Dream and the Case for Structural Keynesianism.

As you read, consider the following questions:

1. What evidence does Palley cite to dispute the "twin deficit" argument?

2. Why is Rubinomics so appealing, according to Palley?

3. What solution to the trade deficit does Palley propose?

Before Democrats can begin to reverse a generation of laissez-faire policy dominance that has put corporations and CEOs ahead of working families, they must debunk Rubinomics, which makes the budget deficit the central focus of economic policy. This focus rests on faulty economics and stands to lock Democrats into confused policy messaging and a path of fiscal austerity that leaves no room for spending on infrastructure, alternative energy or education, among other needs.

The central proposition of Rubinomics—named after former Treasury secretary Robert Rubin, who shaped economic policy under President [Bill] Clinton—is that budget deficits reduce saving and increase interest rates, thereby reducing investment and lowering future living standards. However, the record shows that interest rates have fallen to historic lows over the past several years, a time of large deficits, which fits the common-sense observation that the Federal Reserve largely determines interest rates contingent on economic conditions. Meanwhile, a flood of savings has poured into financial markets from wealthy individuals and pension funds.

Nor does the "twin deficit" argument—that budget deficits cause trade deficits—make sense, as evidenced by the fact that in the late 1990s the United States ran record trade deficits as the budget moved into record surplus. Rather, the trade deficit is due to undervalued foreign currencies and export-led growth strategies by many countries that look to grow by selling to the United States while restricting purchases of American-made goods.

The Appeal of Rubinomics

Despite these logical railings, Rubinomics still has great appeal because Rubin's tenure as Treasury secretary coincided with the 1990s boom. That appeal is misplaced. The rooster crows at dawn but does not cause the sunrise. Rubin was Treasury secretary during the boom, but budget surpluses did not cause it.

The political origins of Rubinomics can be traced back to the 1970s, when conservative charges about big government and "tax and spend" liberals took deep hold on America's political consciousness. Throughout the 1980s Democrats struggled to respond, eventually settling in the 1990s on a strategy of "fiscal responsibility." That strategy was always transitional and defensive, aimed at blunting Republicans' relentless attack on government and plutocratic [benefiting the wealthy] tax cuts. The long-term goal was always an alternative narrative to free-market mythology.

The tragedy is that once a myth takes hold, it must be lived out to be disproved. That is the price paid for losing the war of ideas. This process has now worked itself out, and America is finally grasping the fallacies of market fundamentalism. That creates a historic opportunity, but Rubinomics risks a tragic second act. Rubinomics worked brilliantly as a political strategy in the 1990s. But its success was political, not economic. However, its supporters have lost sight of this and now credit it with causing the late-'90s boom. Consequently, they argue for sticking with Rubinomics, thereby missing the opportunity created by the dismal failure of [George W.] Bush's presidency.

Focus on Investment, Not the Deficit

Instead of continuing down a mistaken path that focuses on the budget deficit, proponents of a progressive economic policy should focus on increasing investment, which is key to productivity growth and full employment. Rising wages and full employment, in combination with a fairly valued dollar, create a favorable investment climate. That sets the stage for a

Deficits Are a Symptom, Spending Is the Disease

There is a mistaken belief in Washington that fiscal policy should focus on lowering the budget deficit rather than reducing the burden of government. This confuses cause and effect. Government spending diverts resources from the productive sector of the economy. That diversion imposes a cost because the higher spending misallocates some portion of the economy's labor and capital.

That cost might be worthwhile if policymakers were funding only the legitimate and proper functions of a central government—such as national defense, a court system, and other genuine "public goods." These types of outlays facilitate the environment in which private-sector wealth creation can take place. But most government outlays fail to meet the "public goods" test. The bulk of government spending today is for transfers and consumption.

This is why it is a mistake to obsess about the deficit.

Daniel J. Mitchell,
"The President's Tax Agenda:
Pro-Growth Measures Jeopardized by Excessive
Spending and Misguided Focus on Deficit,"
Heritage Foundation Web Memo, no. 992,
February 7, 2006.

virtuous circle of shared prosperity. Investment raises productivity, which raises wages and profits, thereby increasing demand and drawing more investment. This is the real basis of a rising tide that lifts all boats. With regard to the trade deficit, the solution is to revalue exchange rates, raise wages abroad so that foreign workers can consume more of what they produce and have countries adopt coordinated policies that stimulate the global economy. That would benefit all, and it is why labor standards must be foremost in trade agreements.

Rubinomics is not only bad economics but also bad politics. First, by arguing that the problem is a shortage of savings, Rubinomics promotes a conservative tax agenda privileging saving and profits, which primarily benefits the rich. Second, by placing budget deficits at the center of the saving problem, it sets government up as a problem and makes a case for shrinking it. Furthermore, by promising to lock Democrats into a path of fiscal austerity, it exposes future Democratic Administrations to the charge of "flip-flopping." This is because fiscal stimulus will inevitably be needed when the current unbalanced boom ends.

Democrats Should Reverse Course

The greatest tragedy of all concerns the potentially disastrous consequences for Social Security and Medicare. These programs are more vital than ever, given America's aging population and retirement wealth inequality. Yet Rubinomics establishes the premise for dismantling them. By claiming the budget must be balanced to increase saving, it sets up a political deal whereby Republicans suspend their unjustifiable tax cuts in return for Democrats putting Social Security and Medicare on the table. This would be the ultimate conservative triumph, the evisceration of the crown jewels of FDR's [Franklin Delano Roosevelt] New Deal and [Lyndon] Johnson's Great Society.

The cruel irony is that Democrats would be the agent of this destruction at the very moment when history is proffering the opportunity for a great reversal of market fundamentalism. At a time of extraordinary productivity growth, due to the maturation of the Internet and other technologies, Rubinomics establishes the premise that America cannot afford these great programs. Most bitter of all, once institutions like Social Security are dismantled, they are hard to resurrect, whereas tax cuts can easily be restored. This means that dealing Social Security benefit cuts in return for a repeal of the Bush tax cuts is both unjustified and a political trap—and [U.S. secretary of the treasury from 2006 to January 2009] Hank Paulson knows it.

> *"We shouldn't focus on deficits them-*
> *selves. What really matters is the*
> *country's balance sheet, its assets and*
> *its liabilities."*

Meeting the Nation's Needs Is More Important Than Balancing the Federal Budget

Joseph Stiglitz

Joseph Stiglitz is a professor of finance and economics at Colum-
bia University; he was awarded the Nobel Prize in Economics in
2001. In the following speech delivered at a 2007 Agenda for
Shared Prosperity event, he disputes the notion that budget defi-
cits should be avoided, or fixed, at all costs. Spending, he says, is
not necessarily negative—even if it means borrowing money—as
long as a nation is spending its money on programs that ulti-
mately benefit its citizens. The United States has pressing social
priorities, Stiglitz says, and these needs must be addressed, even
if it means increasing the budget deficit.

Joseph Stiglitz, "Beyond Balanced Budget Mania," Economic Policy Institute, April 12, 2007. Copyright © 2007 Economic Policy Institute. Reproduced by permission.

As you read, consider the following questions:

1. What example does Stiglitz cite of the U.S. wasting money—and how does he think this decision should be remedied?

2. According to Stiglitz, how did the Clinton administration handle the large deficit it inherited?

3. In Stiglitz's view, why is Sweden's economy so successful, in spite of high tax rates?

B udget debates are a useful way of trying to focus attention on fundamental issues on what the country's priorities are. But they also reflect views of the economy, of economic behavior. I think it's understandable that there should be a lot of focus on the deficit at the current time given the absolute mismanagement of the budget macroeconomic policies over the last six years [2001–2007]. The magnitude of the increase in the deficit in the last six years has been very large.

But as one recognizes that we've had six years of badly managed budgets and badly managed macroeconomics, we have to look at what the realities of our economy are today. And that includes addressing some of the important social and economic priorities.

As we talk about deficits, we have to ask the following question about economic structure. If deficits lead to decreased growth, then a dollar spent on some activity has a cost that is in some sense greater than a dollar. Because we spend a dollar. We don't change taxes. The economy doesn't grow as well. On the other hand, if deficits lead to a stronger economy, then that means the net cost is less than a dollar. And to ascertain that, one has to make a judgment about where the economy is today.

Spending-vs.-Deficit Reduction

There are four propositions I want to put forward. . . . The first is that we should never actually focus just on deficits, but on broader economic concepts. The deficit is only one of several accounting frameworks. And it's probably not the best way of assessing either the fiscal position of the economy or its economic position. I'll come back to each of these four propositions. . . .

The second is deficits may or may not matter depending how the money is spent, how they arise and the state of the economy. The third is that the country has a large number of priorities, real priorities. I'll only talk about three of them, the challenge of globalization, the growing inequality, the health care crisis. But there are others such as our problems of energy and climate change. Meeting these, some of these, will require spending money that might create the larger deficit. And I'm going to try to argue that, in fact, if this money is spent well, it does make sense to do that, even if it [leads] to a greater deficit. And the fourth proposition is that the current state of the economy is such that deficit reduction, done the wrong way, could have a large macroeconomic cost. So that if you put it another way, if we spend money the right way, it could have two benefits, the direct benefit as well as the benefits that come from macroeconomic stimulation.

Maybe I should begin by giving what I think are two further points that are illustrative of these four points that I hope represent a consensus, not of everybody in Washington, but I think of all the right thinking people in Washington.

Reduce Defense Spending, Redesign the Tax Structure

The first is that we as a nation and world would be better off if we ended the war in Iraq and reduced defense expenditure. That not only the expenditures in Iraq, but Star Wars weapons, represent weapons that don't work against enemies that don't exist. And if you waste money, that's a bad thing. [Economist John Maynard] Keynes talked about digging holes and pump priming and argued that even that could be a benefit.

But I think given the list of priorities that the country has, we have a lot better ways of spending money than this particular form of pump priming. And in fact, this particular form of pump priming doesn't prime the pump very much. Because . . . the feedbacks of the re-expenditures don't come back to American as strongly as other forms of expenditure.

The second proposition, illustrative of this general view, is that there are ways of changing our tax structure, raising taxes on upper-income individuals, lowering taxes on lower-income individuals, packages that could reduce the deficit and strengthen the macro economy. So, a redesign of our tax structure could accomplish several of the objectives that I have talked about earlier.

Now, behind what I'm saying right now is a view that the economy is potentially going through a difficult time. I think most people see the economy right now as being weak. The consensus forecasts are that growth in the United States will be slower this year [2007] than it was last year. And even conservative economists see a significant probability of a serious slowdown of the economy. Some people even see a recession. The mistakes in tax and monetary policy that we have made over the last six years are coming home to roost.

Effects of Bad Tax Policy

The mistaken tax policy, the tax cuts of 2001 and 2003, forced the burden of macroeconomic adjustment on monetary policy that led to low interest rates. Low interest rates did not lead to high levels of investments. The nation's balance sheet in a sense was such that people took on more debt. But they didn't spend that debt in productive real investments. In traditional monetary policy, lower interest rates lead to more investments.

So that while there's more public debt, there's also an increase on the asset side. In this particular case, what happened was that people refinanced their mortgages, took out larger mortgages. And it was the real estate sector, both directly and indirectly through refinancing of housing that provided a major stimulus to the economy that helped us to get out of the recession of 2001. But that has left a legacy of indebtedness. And it's important in this not to look at average numbers, but the whole distribution.

And that we are now seeing real problems in the subprime sector. And it's now reflecting in some other sectors that are also risky sectors of the mortgage market. Forecasts continue to be that private housing prices will decline. It will be difficult to sustain the economy. In other words, in the last couple of years, consumption has been sustained by people taking money out of their houses. With house prices going down, that's going to be very difficult to continue, and let alone to increase in a way that would facilitate growth.

Rectifying Balances Wisely

And that is one of the reasons that many people are pessimistic about the economy today. The problem is with that kind of weak economy, fiscal contraction—particularly poorly designed fiscal contraction—would exacerbate the problem and therefore risk the economy having a more significant slowdown than it otherwise would have had.

Now, that means we have to focus a great deal on managing aggregate demand and the difficult problem of rectifying the balances that we accumulated over the last six years. And there are ways of doing it. The example that I talked about before of redesigning our tax structure. We can redefine our tax structure in a way that would address the problem of the growing inequality in our society, stimulate the economy and reduce the deficit. But that will require careful modeling, careful analysis.

In 1993 at the beginning of the [President Bill] Clinton administration, we faced a problem of a very large deficit, much larger than today, and a weak economy. And we designed a package that had the effect of stimulating the economy. But we were very careful in designing the tax policies. We postponed the tax increases, most of the tax increases, until after the economy had recovered. And we focused what tax increases there were on upper income individuals so the impact would be minimal.

As another example, I think stronger expenditures on social programs—strengthened safety nets, more provisions for unemployment insurance—could again enhance growth and stability and help the economy face the challenges of globalization.

Look at the Whole Balance Sheet

Before talking about these challenges of globalization, I wanted to go back to the first point. I wanted to emphasize a little bit more on what deficits mean and why we shouldn't focus on deficits themselves. What really matters is the country's balance sheet, its assets and its liabilities. Consider a company. You would never say, oh, this company is borrowing a lot and therefore, it is a bad company. You would always say what is it borrowing for? Is it for investment? You want to look at both its assets and its liabilities. You want to look at its balance sheet.

And you might also want to look at some of these cash accounts. But you would certainly want to look at its balance sheet. Well, when we talk about the deficit, we're talking about only one part of that balance sheet. We're talking about what's happening to the liabilities, what it owes, but not to what it's spending the money on.

And if you are borrowing money, which the United States has done, to finance a war in Iraq or to finance a tax cut for upper-income Americans, then the country is being left worse off. The balance sheet does look worse. You have a liability, but you don't have any asset on the other side. But if you are borrowing money to invest in education, technology, or, say, the safety net, then you may have a stronger economy. And this is particularly true when you're facing the kind of problem that our economy is facing today.

Sweden's Success

Yesterday [April 11, 2007], I was talking to the former finance minister of Sweden. And Sweden has been one of the countries that has been most successful in facing the challenges of globalization. It's a small economy, very open, with a significant manufacturing sector. In terms of some of the rhetoric that you hear in Washington and elsewhere, it should have been a disaster case. They have one of the highest tax rates. And it's not only true in Sweden: Finland and all the other Scandinavian [countries] also have very high tax rates. If you only looked at tax rates, you would say these countries would be a disaster. And we had a discussion in which the view was that their success was *in spite of*—no, it's not only in spite of, it was *because of* the high tax rates.

Why is that? It sounds counterintuitive. Well, the answer is, it's how the money is spent. Again, looking at both sides of the balance sheet. It was spent in ways that led to a stronger economy, enabling the economy to face some of the challenges of globalization. The net result of this is that, for instance, Sweden and the other Scandinavian countries do much better than the United States on broader measures of success like human development indicators that look at not just GDP [gross domestic product] per capita, but also look at health and longevity in terms of labor force participation. They're doing very well. And they have a sense of social solidarity.

Embracing Change

In a whole variety of indicators, they are doing not only well, but better than the United States. The United States has been, as I say, facing the big challenges of globalization and of inequality. Most of you know the data better than I do. That while US GDP has been growing, median income in the

United States has been stagnating, actually going down in the most recent years. And people at the bottom, salaries have also been stagnating, not just recently but for a number of years.

Globalization necessitates people responding to change or moving from job to job. And in the Swedish model, they responded by providing for active labor policies and systems of social insurance that facilitate people moving from job to job and provide them with security. One of the aspects of success in a modern economy is willingness to undertake risk. And they would argue that because they have greater security, people are more willing to take risk. They've managed their macro economy to have full employment. But not only full employment at low, but full employment at high, wages.

And so they have addressed a lot of the problems of insecurity, not perfectly but far better I think than the United States. And the result is, at least in many of the countries of Scandinavia, a much greater willingness to embrace change, the kinds of change that one needs in a dynamic economy.

Focus on the Short Run

All of this takes money. It doesn't come free. How you finance that, whether you do it out of taxes or deficits, may be of second-order importance. In the long run, obviously, things have to be paid for. Resources have to be paid for. But as Keynes said, in the long run we're all dead. In the short run, we face a situation where we have the risk of a weak economy. And that short-run context involves a combination, I think, of a restructuring of our tax structure that would stimulate the economy more and provide greater equality to deal with the growing inequality that has faced the country over the last thirty years.

This [approach] would allow individuals to take more risk, invest more in education and technology, [thus] assisting active labor market policies that allow people to move from job to job. These kinds of comprehensive investment pro-

Deficits Are Necessary at Times

All economic indicators are now pointing toward a deepening recession. . . .

Under these circumstances, deficit spending is not unwelcome. Indeed, as spender of last resort, the government will probably have to run deficits to keep the economy going anywhere near capacity. . . .

Finally, not all deficits are equal. . . . Deficits that finance investments in the nation's future productivity are not the same as deficits that maintain the current standard of living.

Robert Reich,
"Deficit Shackles: Will January 2009 Repeat January 1993?"
Robert Reich's Blog, October 9, 2008.
http://robertreich.blogspot.com.

grams, I think, can provide the basis of a more dynamic economy that will in fact lead . . . not only [to] greater economic growth, but [to] a more cohesive society.

Finally, let me just say a few words about a couple of the other issues that I think are areas [where] we need to spend more. . . .

Distorted Numbers

The first is that there has been a lot of misrepresentation of the nature of the problems that we face with an aging population. There was an attempt by President [George W.] Bush to scare us about the problems of Social Security. The numbers did not reflect, I think, the real nature of the risk. Obviously, there's uncertainty. There's uncertainty about all the parameters, about growth rates of the economy, growth rates of productivity, migration, all the numbers that go into forecasting a program that's going to be going on for years [into] the future. And those inherently are difficult and uncertain numbers.

But two observations are worth making. The first is that the kinds of numbers that have been used to sell the tax cuts—optimistic, rosy scenarios—are markedly different than some of the more pessimistic scenarios that are being used to say that we face a major problem [with] Social Security. For instance, some of my colleagues told me that if you just adjust the numbers on my [data] migration and make the numbers of migration more realistic, the problems of the deficit and Social Security essentially go away.

The second thing is to put the numbers into perspective. . . . I did [a paper] on the cost of the Iraq war where we conservatively estimated the cost of the Iraq war between one and two trillion dollars. And that provides, I think, a new measure, a new metric, that I use for defining the magnitude of a problem. We could put Social Security on sound financial basis for the next 75 years for approximately somewhere between one-quarter to one-half of an Iraq war.

Real Problems, Real Solutions

So if we can afford the Iraq war, what are we [doing] talking about a serious problem of financing Social Security? It is a significantly smaller challenge. The health care most people think of is a more serious problem. But it's a problem with our health care system as a whole, both public and private. And there are a couple of things within our health care system that we can do that would potentially address again a very significant fraction of the problem.

For instance, we are facing skyrocketing drug costs. And a few reforms, like allowing the government to bargain for prices and creating a pharmacology list of drugs that are more effective like Australia does, would do wonders in using drugs more effectively. So what we need here is social science innovation—not even innovation, to compare with our innovation in our medical sciences—to figure out how to deliver the medicines in a way that is more efficient.

In general, the innovation system that we have for testing and making drugs is a very inefficient system based on monopoly and conflicts of interest, a variety of distortions, which lead to higher prices and, I think, less performance certainly per dollar spent.

A second observation is that practices, standard practices, on a large number of areas differ in various parts of the country. And in ways that are not really systematically related to outcome. And that at least suggests that if you switched from the most expensive to the least expensive practices that are consistent with equally good outcomes, there would be very large savings in costs that would help put the health care system on sound footing.

Climate Change Is a Critical Issue

Now, the final challenge I wanted to just mention very briefly is climate change. I think the evidence that has come out this year has made it even more compelling than it was in the past. I was on the governmental panel of climate change in the 1995 review. And the evidence was overwhelming then. But we made a mistake. We did not expect [it, I think], to play out as fast as it has. One of the aspects in which it's come out much faster is, for instance, we didn't anticipate the melting of the Arctic as [being so rapid].

I should tell a little story that I was in Davos [Switzerland] where all the muckity mucks get together. And at a meeting session, oil executives were talking about climate change. And some of them were saying, you know, you guys are really looking at things in a very pessimistic way. You should look at the bright side of things. And what was that? And they said, well, because the Arctic ice cap is melting so fast, we will be able to get the oil underneath the Arctic sea at a much lower cost than previously we had calculated.

Addressing Climate Change

So there is a silver lining perhaps in every cloud. But the notion ... is clear that the accumulation of greenhouse gases in the atmosphere [represents] a significant risk. If we had many planets, we'd conduct an experiment on this planet and if it comes out the way that almost all the scientists are agreed will happen, we go onto the next one and say, well, we made a mistake. Too bad. That would be one thing. But the fact is we can't go on to another planet. And if we make a mistake here, we have no alternative. And the consequences could be very severe.

It reminds me of a little joke that I heard about two planets actually going around and not bumping into each other, but coming close. And one of them was sighing, saying, you know, things are really terrible with all these humans, you know, the problems. And the other one, [which] doesn't have any problems said, don't worry. It only lasts for a little while. And that sort of encapsulated the problem of global warming.

Some of the things we can do to deal with global warming will actually save us money. Getting rid of the energy subsidies that we have, including the depletion allowances that we have for oil, would save us money. The ethanol subsidies are outrageous. It almost costs as much in oil to get a gallon of ethanol, so the net output of that system is almost negative. We have a 50-cent tax on sugar-based ethanol, for instance, from Brazil. And we give a 50-cent subsidy to American corn-based ethanol. So we have an enormously distorted system. And getting rid of some of these distortions in energy would actually save us money.

Addressing Nation's Needs Requires Spending

But there are other things we will need to spend money on. We will need to spend money on a whole variety of technological innovations to address the challenges proposed by global warming. Research expenditures in this area have actually gone down in the last twenty years. So these are examples of things where we will need to spend money.

In short, what I wanted to say is just repeating what I said before: don't . . . ever focus [just] on the deficit. Look at the broader set of issues. Among the broader set of issues [is] where [is the economy] today? And the economy today, I think, has a certain degree of precariousness where unthoughtful deficit reduction could have adverse effects. I think there are ways of restructuring our tax structures that could stimulate the economy, address some of the most [pressing] problems of growing and equality and reduce the deficit.

But more generally, there is a wide agenda facing our society, important priorities that need to be addressed [and] will require expenditures. And the value of spending has to be weighed against the cost of any deficit. I think there are lots of ways that we can cut expenditures, most importantly in the defense area. But if we fail to do that, it is still almost surely worthwhile spending money in these other areas, even if it has some effect on the deficit.

> "I do not believe it will be sufficient to pay lip service to the long run challenge, while acting only on deficit-increasing responses to the current financial and economic crisis."

The Federal Budget Should Both Meet the Nation's Needs and Eliminate the Deficit

Alice M. Rivlin

In the following viewpoint, Alice M. Rivlin testifies to the Senate Budget Committee that U.S. economic policy can and should simultaneously focus on helping the economy recover from the recession and decreasing the budget deficit. To recover the economy, the United States needs both a short-term stimulus package and long-term investments in public infrastructure. These programs can be paid for by decreasing spending and reforming the tax system. To lower the current budget deficit, entitlement programs must be overhauled. Alice M. Rivlin, the founding director of the Congressional Budget Office, is now a senior fellow in economic studies at the Brookings Institution.

Alice M. Rivlin, "Budget Policy Challenges," Senate Budget Committee Testimony, January 21, 2009. Reproduced by permission of the author.

As you read, consider the following questions:

1. How will a transfer of wealth to lower and middle income people help the economy, in Rivlin's view?

2. According to Rivlin, what are the risks of combining anti-recession and investment packages?

3. In Rivlin's view, why is Medicare an ideal place to start reducing the budget deficit?

I strongly share the [Senate Budget] Committee's perception that the future viability of the United States economy depends on policy-makers' ability to focus on two seemingly contradictory imperatives at the same time:

- The immediate need to take actions which will mitigate the impact of the recession and help the economy recover—actions that necessarily require big increases in the budget deficit

- The equally urgent need to take actions that will restore fiscal responsibility and reassure our creditors that we are getting our fiscal house in order—actions to bring future deficits down.

I stress two sets of *actions* because I do not believe it will be sufficient to pay lip service to the long run challenge, while acting only on deficit-increasing responses to the current financial and economic crisis. Congress and the administration must work together on actual solutions to both problems at the same time.

I will say a few words about the economy and then turn to the question of how to deal with the immediate and longer-run challenges of fiscal policy.

The Economic Outlook

We meet at a time of extraordinary uncertainty about how deep the recession will be and how long it will last. Forecasters all admit that they have little confidence in their ability to predict how consumers, producers, and investors at home and abroad will react to the cataclysmic economic events that have occurred. But people in the forecasting business still have to produce forecasts, so they do the best they can.

The Congressional Budget Office (CBO) forecasts that the recession will "last well into 2009" and that the economy will begin to recover slowly in 2010. CBO expects unemployment to peak at about 9 percent. The CBO is a bit more pessimistic than the Blue Chip [the stock of the most stable and highly-valued companies] average of commercial forecasters, because the rules of CBO forecasting do not allow them to take account of likely congressional actions to stimulate the economy and enhance recovery.

Right now I think we should be skeptical of all forecasts and especially conscious of the risk that things may continue to go worse than expected. The current CBO forecast is much more pessimistic than the one released just last September [2008], and the Blue Chip consensus has been going steadily south for many months. Additional revelations of weakness in the financial services sector could further impede credit flows and produce a continued slide in all forecasters' expectations.

Indeed, uncertainty about the health of the financial sector compromises all current forecasting efforts. The economic models used by forecasters are based on the experience of the post–World War II period, especially the last several decades. Not since the 1930s, however, have we experienced a downturn caused by crisis in the financial sector. Despite aggressive efforts of the Treasury and the Federal Reserve to stabilize the financial sector, credit is not flowing normally, even to creditworthy borrowers. Continued instability in the financial sector and credit tightness could deepen the recession and delay recovery.

U.S. Must Stop Living Beyond Its Means

Also adding to the uncertainty is the fact that before the current crisis Americans were consuming and borrowing too much, while saving too little. We had become an over-mortgaged, over-leveraged society dependent on the inflow of foreign credit. If recovery from this recession is to be solid and sustainable, we must stop living beyond our means. We must transform ourselves into a society that consumes less, saves more and finances a larger fraction of its investment with domestic saving, rather than foreign borrowing. This transformation is necessary, but it will put recovery on a slower track.

Indeed, not since we were a developing country have we been so dependent on foreign creditors. We are lucky that, even though this worldwide financial crisis started in the United States, the response of world investors has been to flock to the safety of U.S. Treasuries [securities such as bonds that are backed by the government], which makes it possible for our government to borrow short-term at astonishingly low rates. But we cannot count on these favorable borrowing conditions continuing forever. Especially if we fail to take serious steps to bring down future budget deficits, the United States government could lose the confidence of its foreign creditors and be forced to pay a lot more for borrowed money. Rapid increases in interest rates and a plummeting dollar could deepen the recession and slow recovery.

Despite the uncertainty of forecasts it is already clear that this recession is bad and that worse is yet to come. Recessions always increase budget deficits as revenues drop and recession-related spending increases. These automatic deficits help stabilize the economy. In addition, since an unusually severe downturn in the economy is threatening, the government should act quickly to mitigate the downslide with spending increases and revenue cuts that will stimulate consumer and investor spending, create jobs and protect the most vulnerable from the ravages of recession.

First Priority Is a Short-Term Package

What we used to call "stimulus" (temporary spending or tax relief designed to jump-start the economy) has been merged into a broader concept of "recovery" and investment in future growth. However, I believe an important distinction should be made between a short-term "anti-recession package" (aka "stimulus") and a more permanent shift of resources into public investment in future growth. We need both. The first priority is an "anti-recession package" that can be both enacted and spent quickly, will create and preserve jobs in the near-term, and not add significantly to long run deficits. It should include temporary aid to states in the form of an increased Medicaid match and block grants for education and other purposes. Aiding states will prevent them from taking actions to balance their budgets—cutting spending and raising taxes—that will make the recession worse. The package should also include temporary funding for state and local governments to enable them to move ahead quickly with genuinely "shovel-ready" infrastructure projects (including repairs) that will employ workers soon and improve public facilities. Another important element of the anti-recession package should be substantial transfers to lower- and middle-income people, because they need the money and will spend it quickly. This objective would be served by increasing the Supplemental Nutrition Assistance Program (SNAP), unemployment compensation, and the Earned Income Tax Credit. Helping people who lose their jobs to keep their health insurance and aiding distressed homeowners also belong in this "anti-recession" package. On the tax side, my favorite vehicle would be a payroll tax holiday, because payroll tax is paid by all workers and is far more significant than the income tax for people in the lower half of the income distribution. Moreover, a payroll tax holiday would be relatively easy to reverse when tax relief was no longer appropriate. This anti-recession package should move forward quickly. Because its components would be temporary, there would be little reason for concern about its impact on the deficit three or four years down the road.

A Long-Term Public Investment Package

The anti-recession package should be distinguished from longer-run investments needed to enhance the future growth and productivity of the economy. The distinction is *not* that these longer-run investments are less needed or less urgent. We have neglected our public infrastructure for far too long and invested too little in the skills of the future workforce. If our economy is to grow sustainably in the future we need to modernize our transportation system to make it more efficient and less reliant on fossil fuels. We need to assure access to modern communications across the country and invest in the information technology and data analysis needed to make medical care delivery more efficient and effective. We need a well-thought-out program of investment in workforce skills, early childhood education, post-secondary education, science and technology. Such a long-term investment program should not be put together hastily and lumped in with the anti-recession package. The elements of the investment program must be carefully planned and will not create many jobs right away.

Since a sustained program of public investment in productivity-enhancing skills and infrastructure will add to federal spending for many years, it must be paid for and not simply added to already huge projected long-term deficits. That means either shifting spending from less productive uses or finding more revenue. Over time, Congress could reduce commitments to defense programs and weapons systems that reflect outmoded thinking about threats to U.S. security, reduce agricultural subsidies, and eliminate many small programs that have outlived theirs original priorities. Reform of the tax system—including making the income tax simpler and fairer, or increasing reliance on consumer taxation—could produce more revenue with less drag on economic growth. None of these policies would be easy, but the resources to pay for large permanent increases in federal spending must be shifted from somewhere else as the economy returns to full employment. Congress will . . . be able to accomplish this real-location of resources [only] if it reinstates some form of long run (say, ten year) PAYGO [pay-as-you-go] and caps on discretionary spending.

Focus on Fiscal Discipline

I understand the reasons for lumping together the anti-recession and investment packages into one big bill that can pass quickly in this emergency. A large combined package will get attention and help restore confidence that the federal government is taking action—even if part [of] the money spends out slowly. But there are two kinds of risks in combining the two objectives. One is that money will be wasted because the investment elements were not carefully crafted. The other is that it will be harder to return to fiscal discipline as the economy recovers if the longer-run spending is not offset by reductions or new revenues.

As this committee knows well, projections of the federal budget show rapidly rising spending over the next several decades attributable to three major entitlement programs; namely, Medicare, Medicaid, and Social Security. Under current rules, Social Security spending will rise rapidly over the next two decades, but level off after the Baby Boom generation passes through the system. The health care entitlements are expected to rise even faster. Moreover, they are expected to keep on rising because they are dominated by continued increases in the spending for health care in both the public and private sectors. If policies are not changed, Medicare and Medicaid—and to a lesser extent Social Security—will drive federal spending up considerably faster than the rate at which the economy is likely to grow. Unless Americans consent to

Both Short-Term and Long-Term Economic Challenges Must Be Addressed

We are in the midst of an economic and financial downturn that many think is the most severe since the Great Depression of the 1930s. Running large deficits now to stimulate aggregate demand will contribute to economic and financial recovery in order to minimize employment and output losses. However, fiscal stimulus measures should not be permanent. Long-term interest rates may rise if a temporary increase in deficit financing is perceived by investors as a permanent large increase in the public debt. Fiscal stimulus measures should also reflect trade-offs between size and longer-run costs from higher debt service, and between size and efficiency. Proper management of any additional spending is critical as well.

The debt being run up now should be repaid when the economy is on stronger footing. While critical now, massive borrowing will add to future debt and make an already difficult situation worse. When the economy has recovered, it is important that we have a credible mechanism or set of policies to ensure that the country pays back the massive debt accumulated during the recession. It is not too soon for policymakers to start the serious policy discussion on what should and can be done to unwind the huge amount of debt we are accumulating now. They should take steps very soon to put a medium-term strategy in place.

Committee for a Responsible Federal Budget,
"Good Deficit/Bad Deficit," www.crfb.org, April 2009.

tax burdens that rise as fast as spending, a widening gap will open up. We will not be able to finance these continuously growing deficits.

Because rapidly rising debt threaten[s] our credibility as sound fiscal managers, we do not have the luxury of waiting until the economy recovers before taking actions to bring down projected future deficits. Congress and the administration should take actual steps this year to reduce those deficits in order to demonstrate clearly that we are capable of putting our fiscal house in order. This can be done without endangering economic recovery.

Fix Entitlements

The crisis may have made Social Security less of a political "third rail" and provided an opportunity to put the system on a sound fiscal basis for the foreseeable future. Fixing Social Security is a relatively easy technical problem. It will take some combination of several much-discussed marginal changes: raising the retirement age gradually in the future (and then indexing it to longevity), raising the cap on the payroll tax, fixing the COLA [cost of living adjustment], and modifying the indexing of initial benefits so they grow more slowly for more affluent people. In view of the collapse of market values, no one is likely to argue seriously for diverting existing revenues to private accounts, so the opportunity to craft a compromise is much greater than it was a few years ago. Fixing Social Security would be a confidence-building achievement for bipartisan cooperation and would enhance our reputation for fiscal prudence.

Vigorous efforts should also be made to make Medicare more cost effective and slow the rate of growth of Medicare spending, which contributes so much to projected deficits. While restraining health-spending growth should be a major feature of comprehensive health reform, Medicare is an ideal place to start the effort. Medicare is the largest payer for health services and should play a leadership role in collecting information on the cost and effectiveness of alternative treatments and ways of delivering services, and designing reimbursement incentives to reward effectiveness and discourage waste. Congress has a history of allowing pressure from providers and suppliers (for example, suppliers of durable medical equipment or pharmaceutical companies) to thwart efforts to contain Medicare costs. The government has also not been adequately attentive to punishing and preventing Medicare fraud. The United States will not stand a chance of restoring fiscal responsibility at the federal level unless Congress develops the political will to hold health providers accountable— whether in the context of existing federal programs or comprehensive health reform—for delivering more cost-effective care. A good place to start is Medicare.

Process Reform

This committee does not need to be convinced that deficits matter and that the deficits looming in the federal budget— exacerbated by the rapid increases in debt associated with recession and financial bailout—must be dealt with sooner rather than later. You know that procrastination will make the hard choices harder and make us increasingly dependent on our foreign creditors and exposed to their policy priorities. The question is: Should you take actual steps now to reduce future deficits or design process reforms that will force you to confront viable options and make choices in the future? My answer is: Do both.

Fixing Social Security and taking aggressive steps to control the growth of Medicare costs would be visible evidence that Congress and the new administration have the courage to rein in future deficits. But the Congress also needs to restore discipline to the budget process—not use recession or the financial meltdown as excuses for throwing fiscal responsibility to the winds just when we are going to need it more than ever. A large temporary anti-recession package is the right fiscal policy in the face of severe recession and should not be subject to offsets—that would defeat the purpose. But more permanent investments in future growth—also good policy—should be paid for and not allowed to add to future deficits.

A Bipartisan Committment to Fiscal Responsibility

Moreover, entitlements, which dominate future spending, cannot remain on automatic pilot outside the budget process. Fiscal responsibility requires that all long-term spending commitments be subject to periodic review along with taxes and tax expenditures. There is no compelling logic for applying caps and intense annual scrutiny to discretionary spending, while leaving huge spending commitments, such as Medicare or the home mortgage deduction entirely outside the budget process and not subject to review on a regular basis. I am a member of a bipartisan group called the Fiscal Seminar (sponsored by the Brookings Institution and the Heritage Foundation) that addressed this problem in a paper, "Taking Back Our Fiscal Future," in 2008. We may not have come up with the right solution, but we certainly identified a serious problem that stands in the way of getting the federal budget on a sustainable, long-run track.

The challenges that face this committee—mitigating the recession, enhancing future growth, restoring sustainable fiscal responsibility—cannot be solved by one political party, but require nonpartisan analysis and bipartisan cooperation. In my opinion they require action on two fronts at once, including a strong anti-recession package and immediate steps to reduce the contributions to future deficits of Social Security and Medicare. They also require agreement on reforms of the budget process that will force the Congress to confront long-run spending and revenue choices.

> "While President [Barack] Obama
> promises a new era of responsibility,
> what he's delivering is a continuation
> of President Bush's fiscal recklessness—
> this time on steroids."

Expanded Government Spending Cannot Be Maintained

Veronique de Rugy

In the following viewpoint, Veronique de Rugy examines President Barack Obama's first budget in light of his campaign promises of fiscal responsibility. While Obama did inherit a large deficit from former President George W. Bush, in order to compensate for it, he would have to eliminate billions of dollars from the federal budget. Instead, his budget proposes millions in new and expanded spending. Rather than fixing the fiscal mess left by the Bush administration, President Obama's first budget suggests he will match, or even surpass, it. Veronique de Rugy is a senior research fellow at the Mercatus Center at George Mason University.

Veronique de Rugy, "The Age of Debt," *Reason*, June 2009. Copyright © 2009 by Reason Foundation, 3415 S. Sepulveda Blvd., Suite 400, Los Angeles, CA 90034, www.reason .com. Reproduced by permission.

As you read, consider the following questions:

1. What kinds of programs will President Obama's increased spending support, according to de Rugy?

2. What positive change does de Rugy see in President Obama's budget?

3. Where does half of the $2 trillion in savings identified by President Obama come from, according to de Rugy?

Beware when politicians promise "fiscal responsibility." It's pretty much a guarantee that every word that follows the phrase will be a lie. President Barack Obama's first budget, entitled *An Era of New Responsibility: Renewing America's Promises*, is no exception to this rule. Every page comes with a promise to end budget tricks and save money by reforming procurement and cutting various types of waste, but the actual plan boosts spending and deploys gimmicks galore. If this is a new era, it's one made of debt.

Promise No. 1: "While we have inherited record budget deficits and needed to pass a massive recovery and reinvestment plan . . . we must begin the hard choices necessary to restore fiscal discipline, cut the deficit in half by the end of my first term in office, and put our nation on sound fiscal footing."

In fiscal year (FY) 2009, the deficit is projected to be $1.75 trillion. This amount is equal to the entire budget of the United States in FY 2000. The deficit represents 12.3 percent of gross domestic product [GDP] and results from the federal government spending $3.9 trillion—an increase of 32 percent over 2008—while collecting less than $2.2 trillion in revenue. Most tellingly, the public debt stands at 58.7 percent of GDP, compared to 40.8 percent in 2008.

It is true, as Obama says, that he inherited most of the FY 2009 deficit. It was George W. Bush, with the support of most Republicans in Congress, who engineered a series of expensive

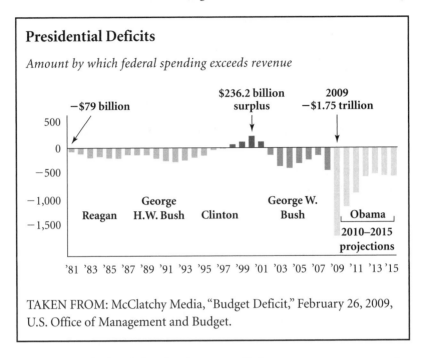

Presidential Deficits

Amount by which federal spending exceeds revenue

TAKEN FROM: McClatchy Media, "Budget Deficit," February 26, 2009, U.S. Office of Management and Budget.

bailouts and the federal takeover of the mortgage companies Fannie Mae and Freddie Mac. But it didn't take long for Obama to add his own billions: $789 billion in "stimulus" (25 percent of which will be spent in 2009), a promise to spend at least another $250 billion to "rescue" more financial institutions, and so on.

An Expansion of the Federal Government

To fulfill his promise of "fiscal discipline," the president would have to shave billions off the federal budget. Yet there are no real program cuts in his budget. Instead the president proposes to dramatically boost health care spending and add many new subsidies for energy companies, students, broadband Internet service, high-speed rail, and low-income Americans.

The result is an expansion of the federal government that will persist long after the current spike of stimulus and bailout spending. Based on government data and Obama's proposed outlays through 2019, ... [there will be a] dramatic increase in nonmilitary spending as a percentage of gross domestic product between 1990 and 2019. In 2019 nonmilitary spending would reach 17 percent of GDP. That's 30 percent higher than at the end of the Clinton years.

And this [projection] understates Obama's vision. First, it includes only a down payment for his forthcoming health care plans. Second, it assumes that "temporary" stimulus spending actually will be phased out. Which is not happening. Take the Environmental Protection Agency: Do we really believe that after getting a 92 percent increase in the "stimulus" and a 33.9 percent increase in 2010, the agency will let its budget increase drop to 0.7 percent in 2011?

President's Budget Not Free of Tricks

Promise No. 2: "This budget does begin the hard work of bringing new levels of honesty and fairness to our government. It looks at a full 10 years, making good faith estimates about what costs we would incur; and it accounts for items that under the old rules could have been left out, making it appear that we had billions more to spend than we really do."

To the president's credit, this budget does contain some positive changes along these lines. For instance, it includes a number of items that the previous administration did not include in the regular budget, such as the cost of the Iraq war.

But the document is not free of tricks. First, Obama told Congress his budget team has "already identified $2 trillion in savings" to help tame record budget deficits. About half of those "savings" come from proposed tax increases. And the administration lists as "savings" until 2019 the annual $170 billion cost for Iraq, totaling nearly $1.5 trillion. Yet even the Bush administration planned on getting out of Iraq by 2012. Cutting spending that was not going to occur isn't saving; it's dissembling.

Unrealistic Economic Projections

The president's budget also claims cuts in discretionary spending by merely shifting several programs from one category of spending to another. One example is Pell Grant funding ($116 billion over 10 years), which is converted from a discretionary program to an entitlement. A recent memo from the House Budget Committee explains that "if these accounting changes were not applied, and the spending continued in the discretionary portion of the President's budget, non-defense discretionary spending would be . . . $18 billion higher in 2009 [than what the administration claims] and $24 billion higher in 2010, and would rise to $34 billion higher in 2019."

Finally, the budget relies on utterly unrealistic economic projections. Obama projects that the economy will be growing by 3.4 percent next year [2010] and by 6.2 percent in 2012. Those figures are several percentage points higher than any other reputable forecast.

That's bad news, because even Obama's doctored projections still show gigantic deficits in our future, dwarfing even the deficits of the Bush years. . . . While President Obama promises a new era of responsibility, what he's delivering is a continuation of President Bush's fiscal recklessness—this time on steroids. Unfortunately, we already know the consequences: slower growth, more unemployment, a lower standard of living, and higher levels of poverty.

Periodical Bibliography

The following articles have been selected to supplement the diverse views presented in this chapter.

Dan Balz "Significant Cuts, or Just a Little off the Top?" *Washington Post*, May 8, 2009.

Massimo Calabresi and Nancy Gibbs "Obama's Rx for the Budget," *Time*, March 2, 2009.

Clive Crook "Phony Budget Tells All," *National Journal*, February 9, 2009.

Economist "Falls the Shadow: The Deficit and Health Care," July 25, 2009.

Randall W. Forsyth "A Dangerous Legacy," *Barron's*, July 17, 2006.

Jason Furman "Fiscal Policy," *Slate*, April 4, 2008.

Peter Grier "U.S. Deficit at Record High and Rising," *Christian Science Monitor*, April 23, 2008.

Terrence P. Jeffrey "Obama's Deficit Charade," *Human Events*, March 2, 2009.

Jeff Madrick "Beyond Rubinomics," *The Nation*, December 23, 2008.

Robert J. Samuelson "The $3 Trillion Cop-Out," *Newsweek*, February 18, 2008.

Allan Sloan "Pain Now, Pleasure Later," *Fortune*, April 27, 2009.

Claire Suddath "Brief History: The Federal Deficit," *Time*, September 7, 2009.

Matt Welch "Obama's Numbers," *Reason*, January 2009.

OPPOSING
VIEWPOINTS®
SERIES

CHAPTER 3

How Should Federal Budget Revenue Be Raised?

Chapter Preface

The debate over how best to raise federal budget revenue often comes down to one central question: whether it is more effective to adjust the existing tax code or to add entirely new taxes. Many political analysts suggest adding revenue by increasing the tax rates on the wealthier members of society. In a 2008 Alternet.org article, Chuck Collins writes, "Congress should boost the top tax rate to 50 percent on annual incomes over $5 million and to 70 percent on incomes over $10 million. This would generate an additional $105 billion a year." While this shift may sound extreme to some, a 2005 *American Prospect* article suggests that a majority of Americans agree that the wealthy should take on more of the federal tax burden: "Gallup's April [2005] survey shows that more than two-thirds of Americans agree that too little of our taxes are paid by corporations ... and 'upper income' earners."

Closing loopholes on corporate tax rates is another strategy recommended by some, to generate more budget revenue. Cassandra Q. Butts writes in a 2004 article for the Center for American Progress: "The news that more than 60 percent of U.S. corporations failed to pay any federal taxes from 1996 through 2000, when corporate profits were soaring, and that corporate tax receipts had fallen to just 7.4 percent of overall federal tax revenue in 2003—the lowest since 1983 and the second-lowest rate since 1934—is an outrage."

At the same time, others feel that tax credits targeted at low- and middle-income earners, such as family tax credits, account for too much lost budget revenue. In a 2007 *Human Events* article, Brian Riedl contrasts tax credits that traditionally benefit the wealthy with those that traditionally benefit less affluent Americans:

The low-income tax cuts reduced revenues the most. In 2007, the increased child tax credit, marriage penalty relief, 10 [percent] bracket and Alternative Minimum Tax fix will have a combined budgetary impact of minus $114 billion. ... But the more maligned capital gains, dividends and estate tax cuts are projected to reduce 2007 revenues by just $36 billion.

In lieu of—or in addition to—these proposals to alter the existing tax code, some economic analysts propose adding new taxes, in order to raise budget revenue. These new taxes vary widely in terms of structure, targeted citizens, and secondary goals. One of the many new taxes proposed is the value-added tax (VAT). Proponent Bruce Bartlett argues in a 2006 *New York Times* blog post, "When confronted by the need to pay for health and other spending programs, every other major country has turned to the value-added tax, or V.A.T. This is the best strategy tax economists have ever devised for raising revenue without investing a lot in enforcement and economic incentives."

Another type of tax that has been proposed by many commentators across the political spectrum is popularly called a "sin tax." This is a tax placed on behavior that the government has deemed undesirable—such as smoking and driving high-emissions vehicles. Many sin taxes are already in place at the federal, state, and local levels. Some commentators argue that broadening these taxes could simultaneously bring in large amounts of revenue for the government and deter certain behaviors. In a 2009 *New York Times* article, Nick Gillespie argues for the legalization of—and taxation on—certain activities currently prohibited by federal law, such as narcotics use and prostitution: "Legalizing vice will not balance government deficits by itself—that will largely depend on spending cuts, which seem beyond the reach of all politicians," he writes. "But in a time when every penny counts and the economy needs stimulation, allowing prostitution, gambling and drugs could give us all a real lift."

Increasing budget revenue is a goal most politicians can agree on, as it allows for more spending on the programs and resources that government deems necessary for a viable society. But the means of attaining this money is something that has been debated since the founding of the U.S. In the upcoming chapter, the viewpoint authors continue this debate, which is sure to be a lively and relevant one for years to come.

> *"Congress is becoming increasingly worried about the [tax] gap ... having cut taxes more than perhaps was wise, lawmakers are really hungry for revenue."*

Federal Revenue Could Be Boosted by Collecting Taxes Currently Owed by Citizens

Albert B. Crenshaw

In the viewpoint below, Crenshaw discusses the "tax gap"—the gap between the amount of money the Internal Revenue Service (IRS) collects each year and the amount of money actually owed. Crenshaw says that the main contributor to the tax gap is the IRS's lack of sufficient resources to fully enforce tax laws. While closing tax loopholes is a worthwhile endeavor, he says, the most effective way to raise federal budget revenue is to collect the tax money that is currently owed. Albert B. Crenshaw writes the "Cash Flow" column in the Washington Post.

As you read, consider the following questions:

1. What is the tax gap estimate cited by Crenshaw?

2. What does Crenshaw suggest the IRS be given additional money for, in order to make tax collection more effective?

3. According to Crenshaw, what was the Joint Tax report's suggestion for improving the effectiveness of the IRS?

To Americans, taxes are a lot like speed limits: necessary in principle for the public good, but when it comes to us personally, well, um, do you see a cop around?

Thus it is that an enduring feature of the economic landscape is the "tax gap," the difference between the amount of money the government collects every year and the amount it would get if people paid everything they owe.

Nobody knows how big this gap is. After all, the perfect crime is one that no one knows took place. That applies to tax evasion as much as to murder. And tax evasion is a lot easier to hide.

One recent estimate put the gap at more than $300 billion annually, but no one has any confidence in its accuracy. The head of the Internal Revenue Service, asked last year for his "best guess" as to the size of the gap, told the Senate Finance Committee he didn't have one.

Congress is becoming increasingly worried about the gap, both for the good and principled reason that failure to enforce laws undermines people's respect for them, and for the less lofty reason that, having cut taxes more than perhaps was wise, lawmakers are really hungry for revenue.

Dissapointing Report

Last year [2004], Finance Committee Chairman Charles E. Grassley (R-Iowa) and ranking minority member Max Baucus (D-Mont.) asked Congress's Joint Committee on Taxation to begin making periodic reports to Congress on ways to close the tax gap. The first of those reports came in last week [January 23–29, 2005], and for Americans who pay what they owe

The Easy Money

Tax increases are no fun, but abiding deficit realities will force politicians to search for revenues, sooner or later. In that event, enhancing tax collections without resorting to increases in tax rates should attract interest. We can only hope that an improved political climate will make it safe for elected officials to advocate a little more law and order when it comes to the bad neighborhood of tax compliance.

Max B. Sawicky,
"The Easy Money," The American Prospect,
June 2005.

and would like to see others forced to do so before lawmakers start repealing legal breaks, it was a disappointment.

While the report did suggest a number of modest changes that would improve enforcement, many of its proposals would simply make compliant taxpayers pay more.

Now, it can certainly be argued that many of the legal ways taxpayers are allowed to reduce what they owe are bad policy, but they are not what cause the tax gap. The tax gap comes from taxpayers who don't pay what they do owe under the law, loopholes and all.

The overriding reason for the tax gap is that the IRS has neither the resources nor the legal underpinning it needs to enforce the law.

The agency's budget hasn't come close to keeping up with the growth of the economy, and that's not even taking into account the increased complexity of both economic life in this country and the tax law itself.

More Resources, Tougher Requirements

So one thing Joint Tax might have recommended was giving the IRS the money to hire more auditors and investigators—at least to the point that the odds of being audited might increase enough to be a credible threat. But of course the committee doesn't view that as its role.

Failing that, it might have made tougher recommendations about records of payments. So-called third-party reporting—the W-2s and 1099s [forms that summarize an individual's annual income] that taxpayers and the IRS get from employers, banks, brokerages and others—has been quite effective in making taxpayers include that kind of income on their returns. The IRS knows they got the money, and they know the IRS knows, so they report it.

But when self-employed people and small businesses get paid, their clients or customers don't have to tell the IRS. The IRS has long known that a lot of this income doesn't find its way onto the returns of the recipients, and it's very difficult for the agency to track down.

The Joint Tax report suggested requiring government agencies, at least, to start telling the IRS about payments they make to contractors and others. But the report said broadening such a requirement to other businesses or individuals would be too burdensome.

And how about capital gains? Two professors, Joseph M. Dodge of Florida State University and Jay A. Soled of Rutgers University, estimated last week in the journal *Tax Notes* that underreporting of capital gains is likely to cost the government $21 billion a year, or $210 billion over a decade.

"On the sale of investments, taxpayers inflate their tax basis and do so with impunity," the two wrote. (Tax basis, generally speaking, is the cost of an asset—the amount a taxpayer subtracts from the sale proceeds to calculate taxable gain.)

Ensure Debts Are Paid

Part of the underreporting is the result of confusion and complexity, but the professors note that "there is effectively no sanctionable duty for taxpayers to maintain their basis records," and courts have allowed taxpayers, in the absence of such records, to estimate their basis.

Dodge and Soled suggest that imposing a recordkeeping requirement and third-party reporting would help.

But the Joint Tax report has other ideas.

Congress could, for example, impose Social Security and other payroll taxes on students working on campus, the report said. It could eliminate the deduction for home equity loan interest, and it could limit the income-tax exemption for short-term rental (15 days or less) of a residence.

It could also extend the federal excise tax on telephone service to all voice and data communications, and it could extend the airline flight segments tax to domestic segments of international flights.

These and numerous other loophole closers may well be good policy. But Congress might find more support for them if it first did more to ensure that everyone pays the taxes he already owes.

> "I am for higher taxes. I am for them
> because I don't think democracy is a
> bargain. . . . It has expensive hopes like
> liberty and justice for all."

To Bring in Enough Revenue to Afford the American Way of Life, Taxes Must Be Raised

Donna Schaper

Donna Schaper is a minister in Coral Gables, Florida. In the following viewpoint, she argues that the typical American desire to pay the least amount of money for everything ends up compromising the American quality of life. For instance, she says, paying less taxes means less road maintenance and inferior schools, which amounts to a diminished quality of life. Schaper says that she is more than willing to pay higher taxes in order to live in a society that provides its citizens with the infrastructure and resources necessary to thrive.

As you read, consider the following questions:

1. What is the difference between frugal and cheap, according to Schaper?

Donna Schaper, "In Praise of Higher Taxes," *National Catholic Reporter*, September 9, 2005. Copyright © The National Catholic Reporter Publishing Company. Reprinted by permission of National Catholic Reporter, 115 E. Armour Blvd, Kansas City, MO 64111, www.ncronline.org.

2. According to Schaper, how are low-income students punished for winning scholarships?

3. What is education really about, in Schaper's view?

My landscape architect just told me she would provide two surveyors' estimates—and she assured me that I could take the one that cost the least. I wondered why she pegged me for a Wal-Mart person, one who wanted a bargain at all costs. Why did she automatically assume I was cheap? Not frugal, but cheap. Frugal is a matter of paying the right price for the right thing. Cheap is different. Cheap pinches pennies until the life behind the pennies is also pinched. Cheap is getting a bargain that turns out, often, to be very expensive.

When it comes to the redesign of my property, I want beauty not cheapness. I am going to be living with this land for a long time. I don't necessarily want the most expensive survey either. What I want is a good survey, something that the great extravagance of my public and private educations will allow me to see, understand, analyze and enjoy.

Permit me to differ with my landscape architect and make myself generally unpopular. I am for higher taxes. I am for them because I don't think democracy is a bargain. I think it is a costly extravagance. It has expensive hopes like liberty and justice for all. We can't afford *not* to pay for these hopes.

Even in "Taxachusetts," the public budgets for health, education and security are pinched. I can't imagine not wanting to spend money on my children's—or your children's—education. Taxes for education strike me as a bargain, an investment with lifelong dividends. The idea that community colleges have to plead for the state to fix their roads or heat their buildings strikes me as a very expensive bargain. Short term, it balances state budgets only to elect politicians whose legacy will be potholes of the road, body, mind and spirit.

Taxes Must Rise

For a half-century, federal taxes have remained fairly constant relative to the size of the American economy—equal to about 18 percent of gross domestic product. But the 18 percent era has to end soon. . . .

It will end because of a basic economic reality.

Americans have made it clear that they want a certain kind of government, one that can field a strong military and also maintain popular programs like Medicare. Yet we are not paying nearly enough taxes to maintain those programs. Even major changes to the health care system—the single most important step for closing the budget gap—will not close it entirely. Taxes must rise, too.

> David Leonhardt,
> *"Like Having Medicare? Then Taxes Must Rise,"*
> New York Times, *February 24, 2009.*

Short-Term-itis

The Wal-Martization of citizenship has the same dangerous case of short-term-itis as most elected officials do. People get hurt in these potholes. Take the ridiculous story of low-income students being charged in transitional assistance benefits for scholarships won. Most people don't know that a low-income student gets into trouble if he or she gets a scholarship. How? That money is counted against their welfare or transitional assistance. Now, there's a bargain for you: Keep a whole generation of people in hamburger jobs. Or consider the consequences of long-term federal debt. We spend; our grandchildren pay.

I know enough about the near sentimentality of how much people with grandchildren love their grandchildren. In many cases, they are actively saving to give them a nice inheritance. Not taxing ourselves in the present, for the present, particularly for wars we choose by presidents we elect, is taking money out of our grandchildren's pockets. If this were not immoral and a perfect example of short-term-itis, it is at least dumb. Or consider what happens when research and development departments get underfunded. Better hybrid cars aren't made. Cures for terrible diseases do not happen. These matters cost the environment and our personal health. There are more ways to look at a family's budget or a nation's budget than just numbers. Cancer costs a lot more than taxes over time.

A Better Democracy

Education is not just about jobs, nor is the environment just about research. Education is primarily about itself, about opening the doors and windows of the heart and mind. The good taxable jobs that result are an important side dish. Every dime we don't spend on taxation today will result in a lesser citizenry tomorrow, both in their own life terms and in the terms of the social order. Employers who resist higher taxes will have only themselves to blame when their next generation of employees can't add, think, imagine or write.

There are workplace consequences to short-term-itis.

Instead of always looking for a bargain and always hiring the cheaper surveyor, as a matter of paltry principle, why not imagine yourself as someone worth something good? Not just the better dress but also the better democracy, as a citizen and shareholder in a country that has expensive dreams?

Internalized Wal-Mart thinking sells our future to the lowest bidder. Wal-Mart surely has a positive place in our world. Applying discount thinking to health, education and welfare, however, is different from applying it to toothpaste. It is not a

121

bargain when the state keeps people in low-income jobs by not giving them an educational leg up.

Here is a new movement for you: Have every low-income person in the country put a sign around her or his neck, "Tax me." Translated, "Tax me" means give me an income, not a handout, so that the tax base can increase. Again morality coincides with common sense: Well-developed citizens make good workers—and increase the tax base.

Cheaping out on taxes is a long-term mistake made for short-term reasons. It is not the bargain it claims to be.

> *"It's time to ... campaign against the loopholes and tax dodges that allow corporations and the well-heeled to avoid paying their fair share of taxes."*

To Bring in Enough Revenue to Match Spending, Taxes Should Be Raised on Corporations and the Wealthy

Robert L. Borosage and Celinda Lake

In the next viewpoint, Robert Borosage and Celinda Lake argue that it is time for Democrats to make a case for increasing federal budget revenue by raising taxes on corporations and the wealthy. The authors contend that the budget deficit is astronomical and the economy is in dire need of public investment, at the same time that polls show that Americans—still angry about President George W. Bush's tax cuts—believe corporations and the wealthy don't pay their fair share of taxes. Robert L. Borosage is co-director of the Campaign for America's Future. Celinda Lake is president of Lake, Snell, Perry, Mermin & Associates.

Robert L. Borosage and Celinda Lake, "Talking Taxes," *The American Prospect*, June 2005. Copyright © 2005 The American Prospect, Inc. All rights reserved. Reproduced with permission from The American Prospect, 11 Beacon Street, Suite 1120, Boston, MA 02108.

As you read, consider the following questions:

1. How do wars and national security concerns generally influence public opinion on taxes, according to the authors?

2. According to the authors, what is the most popular Social Security reform option?

3. Why is the American public so wary of tax-cut promises, in the authors' view?

George W. Bush has made tax cuts the touchstone of his presidency, supporting new ones each year, with the economy in growth and in recession, with record budget surpluses and record deficits, in peace and in war. Most of his fellow Republicans have sworn blood oaths never to raise taxes. They even managed to gain overwhelming popular support for repeal of the estate tax—perhaps the nation's most progressive tax, affecting less than 2 percent of the wealthiest few—by renaming it the "death tax" and peddling a big lie about protecting family farms and small businesses.

Most Democrats, meanwhile, are loath to talk about taxes. "Spend and tax" Democrats sensibly prefer to emphasize the benefits of the spending, not how it is paid for. While President [Bill] Clinton pushed through tax increases on the affluent as part of his first deficit-cutting budget, he focused rhetorically on putting people first and balancing the budget, not on progressive taxation as good policy for its own sake. Later, Clinton and then [2000 presidential candidate] Al Gore championed smaller, targeted tax cuts as a way to counter the Republican call for across-the-board breaks. When Bush was elected, Democrats preemptively embraced a modestly more progressive tax-cut package with a cost only slightly smaller than the Bush plan.

In 2004, [presidential candidate] John Kerry campaigned on rolling back Bush's top-end tax cuts in order to lower the deficit and pay for health-care and education investments. He wasn't hurt by this [platform], but he wasn't helped much, either. His economic agenda was generally overshadowed by the debate on national security and social issues, and taxes ranked relatively low among voters' concerns.

Democrats Must Take Action

Now, with large deficits projected as far as the eye can see and a sluggish economy desperately in need of public investment, Democrats have to figure out what to say about revenue. We simply can't finance activist government without paying for it. Bush and the Republican Congress are pushing to make their tax cuts permanent, while adding billions more in new tax breaks for the wealthiest Americans. And Bush is planning to roll out "tax simplification and reform" this fall [2005], most likely code for a program aimed at further reducing taxes on wealth and corporations—and increasing them on workers and consumers.

In this debate, progressives and the Democratic Party have largely been missing in action. At a time of Gilded Age [a time of great wealth building in the United States during the late 19th century] inequality—with CEO salaries ballooning and corporate America carrying ever less of the nation's tax burden, even as workers' wages stagnate—only a few groups such as Responsible Wealth have issued a populist demand for fair taxes, or for taxing the rich.

But it *is* possible for progressives to make tax equity good politics. The following examination of the public's views about taxes, based on recent opinion polling, lays out the elements of a strategy.

Fair but Too High

General attitudes on taxes are not as conservative as our political debate suggests. No one really likes to pay taxes, but in the wake of September 11 and [amid] two wars, a solid majority of Americans (61 percent to 34 percent) think that the taxes they pay are fair, according to a Gallup poll conducted in April [2005]. Consistent with other times in our history, these numbers reflect the dramatic way that war and national-security concerns influence public opinion. In World War II, Gallup surveys showed that eight out of 10 Americans believed that their taxes were fair. In 1999, near the end of the stable and affluent Clinton years, nearly half of the public (49 percent) thought that their taxes were unfair, while 45 percent called them fair. The polls shifted again dramatically after 9-11.

At the same time, somewhat incongruously, a bare majority of Americans (51 percent) say that they think their taxes are too high, as opposed to the 44 percent who think that their taxes are about right. Nearly 30 percent of those who think that their tax burden is fair *also* say that they pay too much in taxes. But attitudes here have also changed dramatically since 9-11. In 1999, more than two-thirds of Americans thought that their taxes were too high.

Bush's tax giveaways have given Democrats of all stripes occasion to argue against tax cuts for the wealthiest Americans and tax loopholes for corporations. And polls suggest significant public support for progressive taxes. An NBC News poll in April found that 55 percent of respondents preferred a system "like the one we have now, with higher rates for people with higher incomes," while 39 percent favored "a flat tax with the same rate for everyone and no deductions allowed." Similarly, research for the Center for American Progress the same month found 64 percent supporting progressive taxes over 32 percent favoring "the same rate regardless of their income," according to a poll by Penn, Schoen & Berland.

Ask More of Corporations and the Rich

Strong majorities also believe that corporations and the rich aren't paying their fair share of taxes. Gallup's April [2005] survey shows that more than two-thirds of Americans agree that too little of our taxes [is] paid by corporations (69 percent say "too little"; 21 percent say "fair share") and "upper income" earners (68 percent say "too little"; 22 percent say "fair share"), while a slight majority thinks that lower-income people pay too much. Somewhat astonishingly, even a majority of those who describe themselves as upper class or upper middle class (16 percent of the population) agree that upper-income earners pay too little in taxes.

The Center for American Progress poll shows that the public overwhelmingly (by a margin of 77 percent to 20 percent) supports a reform that would "increase the percentage of federal revenues paid by corporate America and close loopholes used by companies to avoid taxes." The same poll also shows widespread support for a range of initiatives to make the tax code more progressive. By 69 percent to 28 percent, for example, respondents favor reform that would cut taxes for middle- and lower-income families while "raising taxes on those making more than $200,000 a year." (Americans are generally wary about "tax the rich" rhetoric, because all Americans want to strike it rich. Using an annual income figure—$200,000 or higher—is more effective.)

The Public Supports Reform

Similarly, in the current Social Security debate, the most popular reform option by far is to lift the cap on Social Security payments and have everyone pay at the same rate on their income. A January poll by Lake, Snell, Perry, Mermin & Associates shows 75 percent of the public in favor of (and 19 percent opposed to) such a plan. Even two-thirds of voters with annual incomes greater than $100,000 say that they support that reform. A strong majority continues to staunchly support this reform, even after hearing the proposal characterized as a steep tax increase.

In any discussion of national priorities, concern about taxes currently falls below worries about the economy and jobs, health care, the Iraq War, terrorism, and education. So on any single tax proposal, opinion is often unformed and fickle. For example, when it comes to income from investments or capital gains, 64 percent of respondents to the Center for American Progress poll thought that such income should be taxed at the same or greater rate than other income, while 28 percent thought that it should be taxed at a lower rate. But a proposal to lower taxes on capital gains and income from investments to encourage economic growth was supported by a hefty margin of 72 percent to 22 percent.

Investments Trump Tax Cuts

Because most Americans think that the government wastes much of the money it is given, tax cuts always have some attraction. People believe that if waste were eliminated, they would not be forced to choose among the investments they want (in health care and education, for example), balanced budgets, and tax cuts. That said, in any discussion of priorities, a majority of Americans do not [place] tax cuts first. Clinton used "save Social Security first" to trump Newt Gingrich's demand for a large tax cut. When Bush first made his case for tax cuts at a time of record budget surpluses, much of the public was skeptical. Polls suggested that people preferred investments in education and health care, or reducing the deficit to save Social Security, over tax cuts. Bush sold his tax cuts by promising that he could reduce the deficit, save the Social Security surplus, make investments in education and health care, and then, "with the money left over," still fund broad tax cuts. (The president has never allowed truth to interfere with his patter.)

Now—with deficits soaring, the president claiming that Social Security is in trouble, and new cuts coming in education and health care—the public is even more wary of tax-cut promises. Asked how to reduce deficits, voters solidly choose raising taxes on large corporations and the wealthy as the best approach. An April poll by Lake, Snell, Perry, Mermin & Associates shows that most voters say that the Bush tax cuts made no difference for their families, and almost half didn't know how much they received. Moreover, the stagnant economy raises people's doubts about tax cuts as a growth strategy. An April NBC News/*Wall Street Journal* poll, for example, found that 54 percent agree that the "tax cuts have not been worth it because they increased the deficit and caused cuts in government programs," while only 38 percent say that they were "worth it because they helped strengthen the economy."

Instead, the public tends to support a broad investment argument over a deficit-reduction one. When it was posed as a choice about what is more effective in stimulating the nation's economy, a *Los Angeles Times* poll in January showed that a solid majority—60 percent—favored a strategy focused on "spending for improvements in the country's infrastructure such as roads, bridges and schools" over tax cuts (34 percent). Respondents were split between a strategy focused on "returning money to taxpayers through tax cuts" (46 percent) and one focused on "reducing the federal deficit and paying down the national debt" (45 percent).

Closing Loopholes, Collecting Taxes

In the early years of the [Newt] Gingrich Congress, Republicans launched an attack against the Internal Revenue Service, holding show hearings about Americans who had been mistreated by the agency. Kicking the IRS seemed like good politics, and Republicans proceeded to cut the agency's enforcement budget.

But with people feeling pressed by rising property and local taxes and worried about service cuts, anger is growing at the way corporations and the wealthiest Americans avoid paying taxes. An April poll by Lake, Snell, Perry, Mermin & Asso-

Increase Takes on the Super-Rich

Considering the magnitude of challenges ahead for America, it seems only reasonable that taxes should rise on the wealthy. Taxing the super-rich is not about class envy, as conservatives charge. It's about the nation having enough money to pay for national defense and homeland security, good schools and a crumbling infrastructure, the upcoming costs of boomers' Social Security . . . and, hopefully, affordable national health insurance.

Robert Reich,
"Why Democrats Are Afraid to Raise Taxes on the Rich,"
Salon, *October 25, 2007.*

ciates for the Institute for America's Future contrasted an argument for collecting taxes against the claim that this would constitute a tax increase that would hurt the economy. More than half (53 percent) of Americans favored shutting down offshore tax havens and closing tax loopholes, compared with 34 percent who considered this kind of tax enforcement to be a backdoor tax increase. Support for tougher enforcement was particularly strong with weakly partisan Democrats (66 percent) and independents (57 percent), and even attracted many Republicans (50 percent).

And when proposals to stiffen tax enforcement are framed as a way to fund investments in Social Security and Medicare or avert cuts in health care and education, 50 percent favored aggressive collection. This argument seemed less attractive to independents, but it earned strong support among Republicans, voters under age 30, those making the least money (less than $20,000 a year), and those making the most ($100,000 and up).

Progressive Opportunity

What's a game plan for progressives? Democrats would be well advised to tie Bush's top-end tax cuts to the failure of his economic agenda. We're four years into the supposed recovery, and there is still a net loss of private-sector jobs. Wages aren't keeping up. Tax cuts for corporations and the wealthy weren't tied to investment here at home. Republican policies created more jobs in Shanghai [China] than in Saginaw [Michigan]. Democrats should say it loudly: If we take some of that money and invest it at home in alternative energy, roads, and schools, we'll create more jobs and more growth and make our economy stronger.

At the same time, Democrats should champion the message that corporations must pay their fair share—especially in a time of war. Close down loopholes, crack down on offshore tax shelters, and ensure that corporations pay the taxes they owe.

In the coming tax-reform debate, the Democrats' argument about fairness should be linked to an argument about economic growth. Simplify the tax code and make it more progressive. Tax income on wealth at the same rate as income on work. Give low-wage and middle-income earners a break while raising taxes on the wealthy and corporations. Invest in areas vital to our economy. That would help generate demand and produce jobs here at home rather than chasing them overseas.

Make a Populist Argument

While Democrats are championing reform and linking it to economic growth, progressives need to drive a far more populist argument. Why not raise taxes on the wealth of the super-wealthy to invest in a fair start for every child, including health care, nutrition, preschool, and the basics in education? We should push for special tax levies on those who make $500,000 or more to invest in basic education and health care.

Already in states as different as New Jersey and Indiana, governors of both parties have backed targeted taxes on high-income earners—in Indiana, the surtax kicks in at $100,000 annual household income; it's $500,000 in New Jersey—to avoid deeper cuts in programs.

Republicans lead Democrats with the public as the party that will hold the line on taxes—and they likely always will. But today's circumstances—America at war with deficits rising, Bush's failed economic strategy—provide a strategic opening for those of us who value greater social and economic equity. It's time to make the argument for public investment in education and the economy, and to link it to a campaign against the loopholes and tax dodges that allow corporations and the well-heeled to avoid paying their fair share of taxes. This would set the stage for contrasting Bush's regressive tax-reform efforts with a bolder progressive tax-reform package, one that would support the investments that can get this economy going.

"America's revenue pyramid is essentially inverted, now balancing precariously on a narrowing apex of top earners."

The Wealthy Already Bear Too Much of the Federal Tax Burden

J.T. Young

In the next viewpoint, J.T. Young argues that the significant narrowing of the U.S. tax base in the past two decades has placed U.S. economic policy in a seriously precarious position. If incomes of top earners continue to drop, or if more of this group were to take early retirement, this would dramatically decrease federal budget revenue. Also, those Americans who bear increasingly less of the tax burden are becoming that much more divorced from the impact of U.S. economic policy. J.T. Young served in the Department of Treasury and the Office of Management and Budget from 2001 to 2004.

As you read, consider the following questions:

1. How did the impact of World War II on the tax code differ from the impact of World War I, according to Young?

J.T. Young, "America's Growing Fiscal Dependence on Its Top Earners," *Human Events*, October 25, 2007. Copyright 2007 Human Events Inc. Reproduced by permission.

2. What common argument do defenders of the current distribution of taxes make, according to Young?

3. What distinction does Young make between the beginning of the modern tax code and the current tax code?

Despite the vicissitudes of U.S. tax policy's last two decades, there has been one constant: an ever-narrowing tax base. Through tax hikes and tax cuts, the goal has been to pluck a shrinking gaggle of geese laying revenues' golden eggs. There is an ironic economics in this growing dependence on America's top income groups at the same time that perceptions of income inequality are increasingly lamented. However that irony should be secondary to the serious concerns about volatility and sustainability it raises for America's fiscal and economic policy.

The Sixteenth Amendment spawned an income tax that now seems quaint in its simplicity and intent. Affecting fewer than 4 percent of Americans, the 1913 law began taxing incomes above $3,000 at 1 percent and topped out at a mere 7 percent. Increased to fund World War I, it shrunk quickly back thereafter.

World War II was a thoroughly different story. Not only was the war bigger, the government was as well. The income tax base broadened to encompass 75 percent of Americans, versus just 5 percent in 1939. And when the war ended, the income tax, like the government, did not retrench.

While the enlarged revenue demands now appear permanent, the income tax's scope has been shrinking over the last two decades' two major tax hikes and two major tax cuts.

A Gradually Increasing Burden

The landmark 1986 tax reform lowered rates across the board but, because rates fell much more for lower income levels (65 percent for those making $10,000 or less versus 2 percent for those making $200,000 or more), the proportion of total income tax paid by income groups above $50,000 rose. The 1990 and 1993 tax hikes concentrated their increases (gross increases of $164 billion and $268 billion, respectively, over five years) on higher earners, increasing the effective tax rates for all earning above $20,000. The 2001 tax cut was similar to the 1986 reform in that its reductions were proportionally greater for lower incomes.

By 2006, the share of income taxes paid by the top 10 percent of earners was 70.8 percent, while the bottom 50 percent paid −0.3 percent—the President's bipartisan Tax Reform Panel stating "taxpayers in the lowest two quintiles [of earners] actually receive more in refunds from the federal government than they pay in income taxes and, as a result, have negative tax income burdens."

Defenders of the current distributional impact often note that income tax is just a portion of the total federal tax burden and that lower income groups face a significantly higher tax burden from payroll taxes. Neglecting this argument's self-fulfilling aspect when lower income groups' income taxes are increasingly favored in tax legislation, 2006 payroll taxes accounted for 34.8 percent of the total tax burden. Yet even when the total federal burden is analyzed, the top 10 percent of earners paid 54.5 percent of taxes and the bottom 50 percent paid just 6 percent.

An Invented Pyramid

Recent American tax policy's distributional trend is unmistakable. Seen from this perspective, it is even easier to understand the clamor over the alternative minimum tax's impending impact. It is not about dollars alone, but distribution. Unless repealed, this alternative tax system, with its severe limitations on tax preferences, would put tens of millions of income earners back on the tax rolls—diametrically opposed to the last two decades' trend.

On Dangerous Ground

The shifting of the tax burden to a small segment of high-income taxpayers is economically dangerous. The beneficiaries of government services are increasingly those who share little or none of the tax burden to pay for them. As they become more numerous, they put more pressure on Congress for more services. Meanwhile, those who bear most of the burden are being squeezed even more, shrinking their number. The result is a growing group of government beneficiaries clamoring for more of a shrinking group's wealth. Congress should put an end to this practice.

Curtis S. Dubay, "The Rich Pay More Taxes: Top 20 Percent Pay Record Share of Income Taxes," Heritage Foundation WebMemo, no. 2420, May 4, 2009. www.heritage.org.

America's revenue pyramid is essentially inverted, now balancing precariously on a narrowing apex of top earners. The economic and political implications of America's inverted revenue pyramid are real and serious. Our revenue stream is certainly more volatile, as seen in the 2000–2001 downturn when falling incomes among top earners (particularly capital gains) yielded dramatic drops.

Economically, more and more of the population is divorced from the effects of the negative economic policy of tax hikes, since they do not pay them. And they are more and more separated from the effects of positive economic policy, since they do not receive them—except through refundable credits. The worst economic medicine of more government spending is encouraged either way. Politically, our Founders would have quaked at the implications of a decreasing minority funding an increasing majority, and it creates a system that is ever more difficult to reverse in a democracy.

Current Distribution of Taxes Must Give Pause

Despite the concentration of the tax burden on a shrinking percentage of the population, calls for its continuation will only grow. From the red meat rhetoric of the 2008 presidential promise-factories to the impending explosion of baby boomer entitlement spending, the demands for additional revenue will grow and the search will begin at the top. Yet the facts of current federal tax distribution should give pause for fundamental questions.

How progressive can our tax code be? The top 50 percent of US earners are now shouldering over 100 percent of the income tax burden when the outlays from refundable tax credits are included. When does progressivity begin to affect behavior? Many of these top earners are also older workers who could take earlier retirement rather than higher tax bills. Such a reduction in high-skilled workers would weaken the economy, because salaries ultimately accrue to productivity, not simply positions.

Today's taxation distribution recalls the modern tax code's very beginning when a small group of top earners bore the brunt of revenue demands. However, there is an important distinction. Then it financed a small government temporarily enlarged by increased spending. Today we have a small tax base financing a large permanent government driven by expanding entitlement spending and soon to get enormously larger. This reality should make us increasingly dubious of politicians' claims for free-rider spending in exchange for top-end taxation. As distributional analysis shows, the most lucrative revenue target is shifting down America's income ladder.

> "As a broad-based tax on consumption
> [the VAT] creates less economic distor-
> tion per dollar of revenue than any
> other tax—certainly much less than the
> income tax."

The U.S. Needs a New Value-Added Tax to Increase Budget Revenue

Bruce Bartlett

In the following viewpoint, former Treasury Department econo-mist and Forbes *columnist Bruce Bartlett argues that the time is right in the U.S. to impose a value-added tax (VAT). Conserva-tives often oppose the VAT, he says, on the grounds that it will encourage rampant spending. But now that there is no hope of reigning in entitlement spending, the U.S. needs a means to raise revenue to match current spending—especially in the wake of President Barack Obama's recent stimulus package and push for health care reform. Putting a VAT in place would be the most ef-ficient means to raise needed revenue, Bartlett argues.*

As you read, consider the following questions:

1. For what purpose was the VAT originally invented, according to Bartlett?

2. According to Bartlett, how has imposing a VAT negatively affected the careers of leaders in several foreign countries?

3. In Bartlett's opinion, why was President Obama's idea to use revenue from a cap-and-trade system to finance health care reform flawed?

According to a *Washington Post* report, the [President Barack] Obama administration and leaders on Capitol Hill are looking seriously at a value-added tax to pay for health care reform and reduce federal budget deficits. Predictably, Republicans reacted to the news with glee. They view the VAT as political poison that will destroy Obama and congressional Democrats if they dare to enact one.

The irony is that the VAT is probably the ideal tax from a conservative point of view. As a broad-based tax on consumption it creates less economic distortion per dollar of revenue than any other tax—certainly much less than the income tax. If Republicans are successful in defeating a VAT, the alternative will inevitably be significantly higher income taxes, which will do far more damage to the economy than a VAT raising the same revenue.

The VAT is a kind of sales tax that was invented by German businessman Wilhelm von Siemens after World War I. The main problem he was concerned with was cascading—taxes being levied on taxes—which was a common problem with manufacturers' excise taxes. The VAT solved this problem by giving producers and distributors a credit for taxes previously paid so double taxation was eliminated.

How a VAT Works

The way a VAT typically works is like this. A farmer grows wheat and sells it to the miller. A tax is paid by the farmer on the sale price of the wheat and is included in the price. When the miller sells the flour made from the wheat, a tax is assessed on that sale as well. But the miller subtracts the tax he paid when he bought the wheat. When the baker buys the flour, he pays the tax included by the miller, which also includes the tax paid by the farmer. When the baker sells bread made from the flour, the tax is assessed once again. But as in earlier cases, the baker gets credit for all the previous taxes paid.

In each case, an invoice trail shows the taxes paid at each step. Those at each stage of production and distribution have an incentive to pay the tax so that they will get credit for the taxes they paid when they purchased goods from other businesses. Thus the tax is only assessed on value added—the difference between what a producer paid for inputs and what he was able to sell that was made from those inputs.

Opinions on the VAT Have Shifted

In the 1960s, Europe began the process of full economic and political integration. One problem that quickly developed was how to prevent domestic sales taxes from creating a cascading effect—goods could be much more heavily taxed depending only on how many countries they passed through. This was considered a serious barrier to free trade. At this point, the VAT's system of having an invoice trail was very attractive because it meant that the tax could be rebated at the border on exports. Consequently, goods would bear only the tax imposed in the country of final sale. Eventually, all members of the European Union were required to have a VAT.

In the 1970s, there was some talk of a VAT for the U.S. Richard Nixon was sympathetic to the idea. But eventually conservatives decided that the VAT's greatest virtue—its efficiency; i.e., its ability to raise revenue at a very low dead weight cost (the cost over and above the revenue collected)—was a defect rather than a virtue. The fear was that a VAT would raise too much revenue, too easily. Better to raise taxes as painfully and inefficiently as possible, many conservatives concluded, in order to limit the government's tax take.

I myself long opposed the VAT on money machine grounds. I changed my mind when I realized that there was no longer any hope of controlling entitlement spending before the deluge hits when the baby boomers retire; therefore, the U.S. now needs a money machine.

VAT Has Had Disadvantages in the Past

Although some liberals have periodically been attracted by the VAT's revenue potential, none have made a serious effort to enact one since House Ways and Means Committee Chairman Al Ullman, D-Ore., floated the idea in 1979 and was defeated the following year, a loss that was widely attributed to his support for a VAT. Forever afterward, Ullman's name has been invoked as proof that a VAT is politically suicidal. In the words of Congressman (later Senator) Byron Dorgan, D-N.D., "The last guy to push a VAT isn't working here anymore."

Politicians are also aware that leaders imposing VATs in foreign countries often suffered electoral defeat as a consequence. After enacting a VAT in Japan in 1986, Prime Minister Yasuhiro Nakasone was defeated a few months later largely because of it. Prime Minister Brian Mulroney imposed a VAT in Canada in 1991, and it was considered the major factor in his 1993 defeat. Although Prime Minister John Howard survived enactment of a VAT in Australia in 1998, his party suffered major losses as a consequence.

However, several factors may now have changed that may make the prospects for a VAT in the U.S. viable. First is the magnitude of the fiscal crisis that will have to be addressed soon. As I explained in a recent column, spending for Social

The VAT's Potential

The VAT [is] one of the world's most popular taxes, in use in more than 130 countries. Among industrialized nations, rates range from 5 percent in Japan to 25 percent in Hungary and in parts of Scandinavia. A 21 percent VAT has permitted Ireland to attract investment by lowering its corporate tax rate.

The VAT has advantages: Because producers, wholesalers and retailers are each required to record their transactions and pay a portion of the VAT, the tax is hard to dodge. It punishes spending rather than savings, which the administration hopes to encourage. And the threat of a VAT could pull the country out of recession, some economists argue, by hurrying consumers to the mall before the tax hits.

Lori Montgomery,
"Once Considered Unthinkable,
U.S. Sales Tax Gets Fresh Look,"
Washington Post, May 27, 2009.

Security and Medicare alone will require a tax increase equivalent to 81% of individual income tax revenue over coming generations.

The Best Source of Needed Revenue

Obviously, the recent explosion of stimulus spending has made the fiscal problem worse. We are already seeing countries like Great Britain having trouble selling bonds and being warned of downgrades by credit-rating agencies. The U.S. is not immune from such problems, which could cause interest rates to skyrocket, at which point a large tax increase will be politically inevitable. The only question will be how taxes will be raised.

Another factor driving renewed interest in a VAT is the Obama administration's push for health care reform. I think it erred by thinking that revenue from a cap-and-trade system to reduce carbon emissions could be used to finance health care. As I explained in an earlier column, a cap-and-trade system is too easily manipulated by the political system and is inferior to a straightforward carbon tax.

This fact is already evident as we see that the House Energy and Commerce Committee has been forced to give away a huge number of carbon credits to buy support for a cap-and-trade bill. These credits are, in effect, tax credits that will both reduce revenue and undermine the whole point of the legislation by allowing politically connected businesses to avoid reducing carbon emissions.

It is also clear that the cost of meaningful health care reform will be much greater than the Obama administration originally calculated. This has led to a search for additional revenue. The Senate Finance Committee and the Joint Committee on Taxation [JCT] have published lists of potential revenues to pay for health care reform that may not be any easier to achieve, politically, than a VAT.

Other Advantages

In a recent study, economist Len Burman makes the point that a VAT is the ideal way of financing health care reform because it addresses a key drawback of the tax—its regressivity. As a sales tax, it takes more in annual percentage terms out of the pockets of the poor than the rich. But if the poor receive health care in return, then this [option] may seem like a reasonable trade-off.

A VAT would also address a common conservative concern about the growing percentage of the population that pays no federal income taxes. In 2007, 43% of all returns had no tax liability, according to the JCT. A VAT would be a way of getting all Americans to pay for the federal government's operations.

Back in 1988, Harvard economist Larry Summers, now a key Obama advisor, explained that the reason the U.S. doesn't have a VAT is because liberals think it's regressive and conservatives think it's a money machine. We'll get a VAT, he said, when they reverse their positions. That day may finally be here.

| "Here's a better idea—and one that will help the federal and state governments fill their coffers: Legalize drugs and then tax sales of them." |

The U.S. Should Implement a Sin Tax to Increase Budget Revenue

Nick Gillespie

In the next viewpoint, Nick Gillespie, editor in chief of Reason .com, makes an argument for legalizing drugs, gambling, and prostitution, and then imposing a sales tax on them. Currently, federal and state governments spend millions of dollars trying to prevent these activities. Gillespie maintains that if governments were to legalize these vices instead, it would put an end to the black market where these products and services are sold. Taxing them would serve as both a deterrent and a source of revenue for the government, rather than an ineffective drain on revenue.

As you read, consider the following questions:

1. According to Gillespie, what percentage of American voters say they support the legalization and taxing of marijuana?

2. Which two states do not permit any form of gambling?

3. Which advantages of the legalization of vices does Gillespie feel are well illustrated by the U.S. history of alcohol prohibition?

The [President Barack] Obama administration's drug czar made news last week [May 13, 2009] by saying he wanted to end all loose talk about a "war on drugs." "We're not at war with people in this country," said the czar, Gil Kerlikowske, who favors forcing people into treatment programs rather than jail cells.

Here's a better idea—and one that will help the federal and state governments fill their coffers: Legalize drugs and then tax sales of them. And while we're at it, welcome all forms of gambling (rather than just the few currently and arbitrarily allowed) and let prostitution go legit too. All of these vices, involving billions of dollars and consenting adults, already take place. They just take place beyond the taxman's reach.

Legalizing the world's oldest profession probably wasn't what Rahm Emanuel, the White House chief of staff, meant when he said that we should never allow a crisis to go to waste. But turning America into a Sin City on a Hill could help President Obama pay for his ambitious plans to overhaul health care and invest in green energy. More taxed vices would certainly lead to significant new revenue streams at every level. That's one of the reasons 52 percent of voters in a recent Zogby poll said they support legalizing, taxing and regulating the growth and sale of marijuana. Similar cases could be made for prostitution and all forms of gambling.

In terms of economic stimulation and growth, legalization would end black markets that generate huge amounts of what economists call "deadweight losses," or activity that doesn't contribute to increased productivity. Rather than spending precious time and resources avoiding the law (or, same thing, paying the law off), producers and consumers could more easily get on with business and the huge benefits of working and playing in plain sight.

Billions in Revenue

Consider prostitution. No reliable estimates exist on the number of prostitutes in the United States or aggregate demand for their services. However, Nevada, one of the two states that currently allows paid sex acts, is considering a tax of $5 for each transaction. State Senator Bob Coffin argues further that imposing state taxes on existing brothels could raise $2 million a year (at present, brothels are allowed only in rural counties, which get all the tax revenue), and legalizing prostitution in cities like Las Vegas could swell state coffers by $200 million annually.

A conservative extrapolation from Nevada to the rest of the country would easily mean billions of dollars annually in new tax revenues. Rhode Island, which has never explicitly banned prostitution, is on the verge of finally doing so—but with the state facing a $661 million budget shortfall, perhaps fully legalizing the vice (and then taking a cut) would be the smarter play.

Every state except Hawaii and Utah already permits various types of gambling, from state lotteries to racetracks to casinos. In 2007, such activity generated more than $92 billion in receipts, much of which was earmarked for the elderly and education. Representative Barney Frank, Democrat of Massachusetts, has introduced legislation to repeal the federal ban on online gambling; and a 2008 study by PriceWaterhouseCoopers estimates that legalizing cyberspace betting alone could yield as much as $5 billion a year in new tax revenues. Add to that expanded opportunities for less exotic forms of wagering at, say, the local watering hole and the tax figure would be vastly larger.

The Morality of Sin Taxes

Behavior expresses our morality. Taxes influence moral choices through the use of incentives and admonishments. Sin taxes are a special case of consumption or sales taxes. "Sin taxes" is a popular term that refers to government levies on pleasure or human indulgence, for example, smoking cigarettes or drinking alcohol. Sin taxes can be defined as those government revenues garnered from the purchase of services or the consumption of resources that generally exhibit three characteristics. First, the behavior exhibits an inelastic demand curve; the behavior is addictive. Second, the behavior is self-destructive or harmful to the individual, with immediate or long-term personal negative consequences, for example, death, obesity. Third, the behavior is harmful to others; it generates negative externalities, for example, polluting the air.

Leaders attempt to use and influence our moral behavior. Prosocial behavior is desirable, moral; antisocial behavior is not. Prosocial behaviors may be an antidote to antisocial behaviors. More important, prosocial leadership and leader behaviors can offer a constructive social path for pursuing and achieving the common good, through skilled leadership and a positive work ethic of wealth creation.

Peter Lorenzi,
"The Moral Grounds of Sin Taxes," Society, vol. 44, no. 1,
November/December 2006.

Prohibition Doesn't Work

Based on estimates from the White House Office of National Drug Control Policy, Americans spend at least $64 billion a year on illegal drugs. And according to a 2006 study by the former president of the National Organization for the Reform of Marijuana Laws, Jon Gettman, marijuana is already the top cash crop in a dozen states and among the top five crops in 39 states, with a total annual value of $36 billion.

A 2005 cost-benefit analysis of marijuana prohibition by Jeffrey Miron, a Harvard economist, calculated that ending marijuana prohibition would save $7.7 billion in direct state and federal law enforcement costs while generating more than $6 billion a year if it were taxed at the same rate as alcohol and tobacco. The drug czar's office says that a gram of pure cocaine costs between $100 and $150; a gram of heroin almost $400; and a bulk gram of marijuana between $15 and $20. Those transactions are now occurring off the books of business and government alike.

As the history of alcohol prohibition underscores, there are also many non-economic reasons to favor legalization of vices: Prohibition rarely achieves its desired goals and instead increases violence (when was the last time a tobacco kingpin was killed in a deal gone wrong?) and destructive behavior (it's hard enough to get help if you're a substance abuser and that much harder if you're a criminal too). And by policing vice, law enforcement is too often distracted at best or corrupted at worst, as familiar headlines about cops pocketing bribes and seized drugs attest. There's a lot to be said for treating consenting adults like, well, adults.

An Economic Lift

But there is an economic argument as well, one that Franklin Roosevelt understood when he promised to end Prohibition during the 1932 presidential campaign. "Our tax burden would not be so heavy nor the forms that it takes so objectionable," thundered Roosevelt, "if some reasonable proportion of the unaccountable millions now paid to those whose business had been reared upon this stupendous blunder could be made available for the expense of government."

Roosevelt could also have talked about how legitimate fortunes can be made out of goods and services associated with vice. Part of his family fortune came from the opium trade, after all, and he and other leaders during the Depression oversaw a generally orderly re-legalization of the nation's breweries and distilleries.

There's every reason to believe that today's drug lords could go legit as quickly and easily as, say, Ernest and Julio Gallo, the venerable winemakers who once sold their product to Al Capone. Indeed, here's a (I hope soon-to-be-legal) bet worth making: If marijuana is legalized, look for the scion of a marijuana plantation operation to be president within 50 years.

Legalizing vice will not balance government deficits by itself—that will largely depend on spending cuts, which seem beyond the reach of all politicians. But in a time when every penny counts and the economy needs stimulation, allowing prostitution, gambling and drugs could give us all a real lift.

| "*The temptation to impose sin taxes is one that should be resisted for economic and moral reasons.*"

The U.S. Should Not Implement a Sin Tax

Robert A. Sirico

In the viewpoint below, Robert A. Sirico discusses the possibility of a sin tax being imposed on sugary foods to pay for President Barack Obama's health care reform. While a new source of revenue is obviously appealing, he says, numerous studies demonstrate that sin taxes do not actually discourage undesirable behaviors; in some cases, they actually encourage them. Furthermore, there are much more effective—and morally consistent—means of persuading citizens to live healthier lifestyles than government interference. Robert A. Sirico is a Roman Catholic priest, and he is president and co-founder of the Acton Institute for the Study of Religion and Liberty.

As you read, consider the following questions:

1. What national epidemic is a tax on sugary soft drinks intended to curb?

2. What other large American industry is "Big Food" compared to in the article?

3. What values cherished by Americans do Brownell and Warner only "grudgingly acknowledge," according to Sirico?

D ramatically expanding the reach of the federal government by adding new "universal" entitlements, while at the same time pretending to manage the economy out of the pit of a severe economic downturn, is no mean feat. Which is why the sin tax, an excise tax on those goods that elected officials deem morally suspect, has come roaring back.

On May 18 [2009], *Politico* reported that the Senate Finance Committee was looking for ways to pay for President Barack Obama's "sweeping health reform overhaul" by "slapping an excise tax on 'sugar-sweetened beverages' for the first time, and imposing a uniform tax across wine, beer, and liquor, which are currently taxed at different levels." According to the Congressional Budget Office, a tax of 3 cents per 12-ounce serving of soft drink (like the 18 percent tax on sugary drinks that New York Gov. David Paterson recently failed to push through) would generate $24 billion over four years.

What's behind this is the notion that sugary soft drinks are one of the chief culprits of a national epidemic of obesity. According to the Centers for Disease Control and Prevention, obesity rates doubled among adults between 1980 and 2000. About 60 million adults, or 30 percent of the adult population, are now obese.

The New Puritans

The elite media, liberal think tanks, and academic researchers are already building a case against Big Food [manufacturers of edibles] for its scarlet sins: sweetened drinks, fatty snacks, alcoholic beverages. You know what's coming next: a wave of punitive government regulation and scores of lawsuits aiming to shake down the nation's vast food and beverage industry. It's the same strategy developed for the assault on the tobacco industry—tax the bad stuff out of existence. Today, in New York City, the price of a pack of cigarettes now tops $9 (each pack now carries $5.26 in taxes), which makes the city one of the most expensive places in the country to smoke.

Never mind if you have freely chosen to smoke a cigarette or drink a cold Coke on a hot summer's day. . . . The New Puritans who are ready to dramatically expand the welfare state and limit personal freedoms claim to know what's best for you.

The sin tax seems like a convenient ploy when the state is searching for new sources of revenue in fiscally tight times. A sin tax also appeals to some voters who view it as a way of discouraging consumption of certain objectionable products. Yet the temptation to impose sin taxes is one that should be resisted for economic and moral reasons. The consequences of the sin tax are often the very opposite of those intended by its designers. Rather than increasing revenue, the sin tax can reduce it. Rather than discouraging what are regarded as morally questionable behaviors, the sin tax can make them more appealing. Rather than reducing what are perceived to be internal costs of the sin, the sin tax can increase them and expand them to society as a whole.

A Failed Policy Approach

The evidence that sin taxes are a failed policy approach is incontrovertible. According to a new report from the Mercatus Center, "taxes on sugar-sweetened soft drinks do not necessarily advance the overall public interest, may be regressive in nature, and hardly ever work as intended." The bottom line, say researchers Richard Williams and Katelyn Christ, is that a convincing body of evidence tells us that boosting food and drink prices "is not sufficient to make 'fat taxes' a viable tool to lower obesity." That's because soft drinks are really a small portion of most people's diets.

Don't Raise Revenue on the Backs of the Poor

A government needs revenues. So what does it do? It taxes the poor. That happens too often, says Michael Davis, a senior fellow at the National Center for Policy Analysis (NCPA) in Dallas. "It's politically expedient." . . .

One frequent way the poor get hit is additional "sin taxes"—taxes placed on gambling, tobacco, and alcoholic beverages. Because the poor tend to consume more of these items per capita than do those who are better off, poorer people bear a disproportionate share of that tax burden.

David R. Francis,
"The Poor Need Help, Not Hidden Taxes,"
Christian Science Monitor, *July 9, 2007.*

The Mercatus report also points to something that all taxpayers should be aware of: secretive revenue shifting by those levying the tax. Williams and Christ point to an Arkansas soft drink tax passed in 1992 that was supposed to pour money into the state's Medicaid program. However, when there was an attempt to repeal the tax, taxpayers discovered that policy makers were diverting the revenue to the general fund. It happens time and again.

Yet, the advocates of new sin taxes to support a growing American welfare state go heedlessly marching on. In Senate testimony on May 12 [2009], Michael F. Jacobson of the Washington-based Center for Science in the Public Interest asked for "strong, specific prevention measures" to cure obesity, including raising taxes on alcoholic beverages, taxing soft drinks, and banning trans fats. He asked Congress to impose an excise tax on non-diet soft drinks, both carbonated and non-carbonated. A tax of one cent per 12 ounces would raise about $1.5 billion annually; a tax of one cent per ounce would raise about $16 billion per year, reduce consumption, and slow rising rates of obesity, he testified. Each penny tax per 12 ounces would reduce consumption by about 1 percent, Jacobson claimed.

Big Food and Big Tobacco

In "Blaming the Food Industry for Obesity," *BusinessWeek* blogger Cathy Arnst recently reported that "two new studies conclude that the food industry is following the tobacco industry's play book to ensure that we keep loading up on calories, and as a result virtually all of the weight gain in the U.S. over the last 30 years can be attributed to eating more, not moving less."

Arnst also quotes a study by two university researchers who tipped their hand when they titled their work: "The Perils of Ignoring History: Big Tobacco Played Dirty and Millions Died. How Similar Is Big Food?" Researchers Kelly D. Brownell and Kenneth E. Warner concluded that although there are differences between tobacco and food (a startling insight for sure) there are "significant similarities in the actions that these industries have taken in response to concern that their products cause harm. Because obesity is now a major global problem, the world cannot afford a repeat of the tobacco history, in which industry talks about the moral high ground but does not occupy it."

Brownell and Warner also grudgingly acknowledged that personal responsibility and freedom are values cherished by Americans, but "they obscure the reality that some of the most significant health advances have been made by population-based public health approaches in which the overall welfare of the citizenry trumps certain individual or industry freedoms." In other words, the government knows better than you do how to feed and raise your children.

155

New Opportunities for Legal Action

Who, or what exactly, is Big Food? Brownell and Warner observe that, unlike the tobacco industry, the food industry is larger and more fragmented. If you are a trial lawyer looking for new and bountiful vistas of tort action, Big Food must look extremely tempting:

> The industry is diverse and fragmented in some ways, counting as its players a local baker making bread for a few stores; a family running a convenience store; an organic farmer; mega companies like Kraft, McDonald's, and Coca-Cola; and even Girl Scouts selling cookies. The same company making fried foods laden with saturated fat might also sell whole-grain cereal.

> In other ways, the industry is organized and politically powerful. It consists of massive agribusiness companies like Cargill, Archer Daniels Midland, Bunge, and Monsanto; food sellers as large as Kraft (so big as to own Nabisco) and Pepsi-Co (owner of Frito-Lay); and restaurant companies as large as McDonald's and Yum! Brands (owner of Pizza Hut, Taco Bell, KFC [Kentucky Fried Chicken], and [others]). These are represented by lobbyists, lawyers, and trade organizations that in turn represent a type of food (e.g., Snack Food Association, American Beverage Association), a segment of the industry (e.g., National Restaurant Association), a constituent of food (e.g., Sugar Association, Corn Refiners Association), or the entire industry (e.g., Grocery Manufacturers of America).

Discourage Behavior by Other Means

It must be noted that there is a certain irony in the fact that some of the very advocates of sin taxes are those often heard, in other contexts, making comparisons between religious conservatives and the Taliban while insisting that the government "keep your laws off our bodies."

It's time to stop this nonsense. Whatever economic or social benefits one can dream up from the sin tax, we must also realize that the decision to tax must be weighed against the social benefits for reducing the behavior by slow and deliberate persuasion and voluntary action. When it comes to public policy, the preferred method of discouraging sin should fall under the category of alternative, mediating institutions, notably family, church and school. That would leave government officials more time to focus on the sins they can really do something about—their own.

Periodical Bibliography

The following articles have been selected to supplement the diverse views presented in this chapter.

Gary Bauer   "Secularism's Sin Taxes," *Human Events*, May 14, 2009.

Matthew Continetti   "A Big, Fat Failure," *Weekly Standard*, April 6, 2009.

Thomas R. Eddlem   "A New Era of Irresponsibility," *New American*, March 30, 2009.

Stephen J. Entin   "The Folly of 'Family Friendly' Tax Policy," *Wall Street Journal*, April 9, 2008.

Justin Fox   "Thanks, Rich People!" *Time*, March 19, 2007.

Robert H. Frank   "Why Wait to Repeal Tax Cuts for the Rich?" *New York Times*, December 5, 2008.

John Steele Gordon   "The Economic Contradictions of Obama-ism," *Commentary*, April 2009.

John Maggs   "The Vanishing Taxpayer," *National Journal*, April 22, 2006.

Rob Moll   "Death Tax Resurrected," *Christianity Today*, April 2009.

National Review   "Tax and Spin," March 23, 2009.

Kristina Rasmussen   "Ten Tax-Hike Threats in 111th Congress," *Human Events*, January 26, 2009.

Sheldon Richman   "Why Cut Taxes?" *Freeman*, October 2006.

Jeffrey D. Sachs   "Paying for What Government Should Do," *Scientific American*, May 2009.

Nate Silver   "Republicans: Raise Taxes," *Esquire*, September 2009.

CHAPTER 4

How Should Federal Budget Money Be Spent?

Chapter Preface

On the U.S. political spectrum, Democrats are often associated with "liberal" priorities and positions and Republicans are associated with "conservative" priorities and positions. In terms of fiscal policy, Democrats are seen as spenders who view government's primary role as making sure the country's needs are met, through social programs such as Medicaid and Social Security. Republicans are known to be "fiscally conservative" and to prefer a more limited government role in social policy and the everyday lives of citizens. This dichotomy was radically challenged with the two-term presidency of George W. Bush. In the McClatchy newspapers, David Lightman writes in 2007, "George W. Bush, despite all his recent bravado about being an apostle of small government and budget-slashing, is the biggest spending president since Lyndon B. Johnson. In fact, he's arguably an even bigger spender than LBJ." In a 2005 *Wall Street Journal* op-ed piece, conservative commentator Peggy Noonan agrees: "George W. Bush is a big spender. He has never vetoed a spending bill. When Congress serves up a big slab of fat, crackling pork, Mr. Bush responds with one big question: Got any barbecue sauce?"

President Bush's proficiency for spending has, by many accounts, shaken the very identity of the Republican Party. In his 2004 *Reason* article, "Ten Reasons to Fire George W. Bush," Jesse Walker writes, "We all expect a Republican president to molest our civil liberties. But this one has poached the Democrats' turf as well, increasing federal spending by over $400 billion—its fastest rate of growth in three decades." Walker explicitly compares Bush to his Democratic predecessor: "Under Bush, domestic discretionary spending has already gone up 25 percent. ([President Bill] Clinton only increased it 10 percent, and it took him eight years to do that.)" Nick

Gillespie and Veronique de Rugy write in a 2005 article in the same magazine, "After five years of Republican reign, it's time for small-government conservatives to acknowledge that the GOP has forfeited its credibility when it comes to spending restraint." In short, Bush's spending behavior seems to have called into question a central aspect of the traditional Republican Party platform—fiscal restraint—and, by extension, the Republican/Democrat dichotomy that has ordered American politics for so long.

More recently, some say that the current president, Barack Obama, is quickly reinstating the traditional political model. Within the first two months of his presidency, President Obama signed into law an economic stimulus package that totaled $787 billion. Stephen Clark of Fox News called this package "the largest expansion of federal government since World War II." In response, the same conservative commentators that protested the Bush administration's fiscal policies began speaking out again—though, arguably, with less of a sense of betrayal. In his 2009 *Bloomberg News* article, Kevin Hassett writes:

Obama is not the anti-Bush. He is Bush on steroids.

Bush's policies could be summarized in one sentence: Spend like a drunken sailor and don't pay for it. Obama's policies can be summarized by the same sentence, except that Obama goes beyond drunk to alcohol poisoning.

While conservatives may be displeased with President Obama's spending behaviors so far, they might at least feel at ease that his spending lines up with his party affiliation.

No matter who is in the White House—or Congress—and no matter what their political party, the debates over how much government should spend, and on what, will continue. In the chapter that follows, political commentators of various stripes discuss the spending patterns of past and current elected officials, and the authors debate how these patterns might be adjusted to better reflect national priorities.

| "Resources must match our security strategy. Anything less is a compromise the nation cannot afford."

Federal Defense Spending Should Be Increased

Valerie Lynn Baldwin

In the viewpoint below, Valerie Lynn Baldwin, assistant secretary of the Army for financial management and comptroller, argues that if defense spending does not increase, there could be disastrous consequences. The damage caused by Hurricane Katrina was partly due to the Army Corps of Engineers not receiving enough money to maintain the levees. In the case of national defense, insufficient funding has already affected troop readiness, and it will eventually diminish the military's ability to recruit volunteers. Ultimately, Baldwin writes, defense spending should be determined by what is needed to carry out defense strategy—rather than the other way around.

As you read, consider the following questions:

1. What were the personnel requirements for executing military strategy set by the Quadrennial Defense Review (QDR) in 2006?

Valerie Lynn Baldwin, "The Cost of the Army," *Army*, vol. 56, October 2006, pp. 43–45.

2. How much of the gross domestic product (GDP) is put toward national defense, according to Baldwin?

3. How much does Baldwin think should be given to the military in the 2008 budget?

A year after Hurricane Katrina swept over the Gulf Coast and devastated the city of New Orleans [in 2005], the United States is still calculating the damage and cost to the regional and national economies. Today [2006], unemployment in New Orleans remains higher than before Katrina, and the local workforce is about 190,000 people smaller. Many estimate that insured and uninsured damages will top $200 billion. That figure does not cover the cost of diverting federal, state and local resources from other uses to hurricane recovery; nor can it account for the loss of more than 1,300 people.

Everyone knew the 200-year storm, as Katrina has been dubbed, was a possibility—even a probability. Why then has the toll been so terrible from this one storm? Among the factors that contributed to this outcome was a persistent funding problem. For decades, civil works projects that could have softened Katrina's impact were not given adequate resources. In each budget cycle, the Army Corps of Engineers received less money than it needed, despite the risk. There was always next year to tackle the problem.

The Katrina experience offers an important lesson that can be applied to the Defense Department and the Army: Consistently underfunding legitimate requirements can lead to disaster. In the case of the military, not providing enough money holds terrible implications for national security and national survival. Resources must match our security strategy. Anything less is a compromise the nation cannot afford.

Determining True Cost

So, how much should the nation spend on Defense? That is the proverbial $64,000 question. Why isn't there a quick, easy answer? Until recently, none of the military services had done an accurate assessment of its true cost. Determining true cost goes beyond looking at the balance sheet at the end of the year to see how much was spent. For a variety of reasons, that figure is not representative of the real cost. Cost estimates produced to date take everything everyone wants—what sometimes are erroneously labeled as requirements—and throw it all into a model generator, which eventually spits out a number. Though done in good faith, model-driven estimates never capture reality.

How should real costs be established? By ascertaining the amount of resources necessary to fulfill the U.S. security strategy. The 2006 Quadrennial Defense Review (QDR) sets the capability baseline for executing that strategy. For the Army to meet the QDR's requirements, it must maintain 70 brigade combat teams: 42 in the active component and 28 in the National Guard. Eighteen of these teams must be ready to deploy at any time, and another 18 must be sufficiently prepared to surge almost immediately after the first 18. Of course, these units, as well as all of the needed support elements, must be fully staffed, equipped and trained.

With these capabilities as the driver, the Army this year produced a reasonably accurate cost figure for itself. The Army needs $130 billion annually in fiscal year (FY) 2006 dollars to accomplish the mission laid out in the QDR. This amount, of course, excludes any and all unplanned and contingency activities, including prosecution of the global war on terrorism. Various entities, including the program evaluation groups and outside observers, have reviewed this assessment and concluded that the $130 billion requirement is correct.

Readiness Requires Adequate Resources

The FY 2007 budget request for the Army was $112 billion. Compare the cost of the Army to the funding sought and a strategy-resources mismatch appears. Add in the incremental costs of fighting the global war on terrorism—approximately another $67 billion per year—and the mismatch becomes even starker.

This disparity is dangerous and cannot continue. Already, Army readiness is declining and it will drop further as long as the status quo remains. Eventually, the lack of adequate funding will have an impact on the Army's ability to recruit and retain an all-volunteer force. We as a nation thus have an incredibly significant choice to make: Should costs drive policy or should policy drive our costs? If we elect the former, then the QDR strategy must be revised and we must rethink today's operational reality. If we decide upon the latter, then we must direct more financial resources toward the Army, and probably the Marine Corps, as well.

The Defense Department's 200-year storm is coming. The global war on terrorism will continue for quite some time. A major contingency operation is not out of the question; in fact, the United States likely will face a significant conflict against a more traditional adversary sooner than the general public would imagine. The United States must be prepared not only to manage such a situation diplomatically but to prevail militarily.

The Price of Insufficient Funding

The amount of investment required is moderate, and even quite small when viewed in proportion to Gross Domestic Product (GDP). The United States is putting the equivalent of 3.9 percent of GDP toward national defense. The Army only receives the equivalent of 1.1 percent—and that figure includes supplemental appropriations, which have equaled about two-thirds of the Army's baseline budget requests. Without supplemental, the Army's budget amounts to just slightly more than one-third of 1 percent of GDP. At these levels, defense spending as a percentage of GDP is at its lowest point in 60 years—despite operational conditions that have not been seen since World War II.

To cover the base cost of the Army in FY 2008, the nation must provide $139 billion, a $27 billion increase above the initial request for FY 2007. This boost is not small, but failure to meet the requirement would come at an even greater price. Do we dare take the gamble that we will have another year—and maybe another and another—to get it right, as happened in New Orleans? Or do we lower our risk as much as possible and ensure our ability to protect the United States' security, prosperity and future? The choice is ours.

*"A look at the defense budget shows that
we're building a new military while still
paying for the old one."*

Federal Defense Spending
Should Be Cut

James Surowiecki

*In the following viewpoint, New Yorker "Financial Page" writer
James Surowiecki decries the current state of defense spending.
While half of the federal government's discretionary spending
goes to the military, far too little of this money goes to meeting
immediate needs such as body armor for soldiers in Iraq. Instead, for example, billions are spent on high-tech weapons systems designed to fight old enemies like the Soviet Union. Aside
from its being fiscally irresponsible, such spending actually makes
the United States less safe, he says. Ultimately, the George W.
Bush administration's pattern of giving the Defense Department
a blank check needed to change.*

As you read, consider the following questions:

1. How much higher was the defense budget at the time of
   this article versus in 2001?

2. In Surowiecki's view, why had Pentagon waste and inefficiency become so much worse in the five years prior to this article?

3. What point does Surowiecki hope to make using the M&M's analogy?

A couple of weeks ago [July 2006], the Senate Appropriations Committee did something unusual: It actually said no to the Defense Department, trimming next year's requested defense budget by a small amount. In practice, the cuts will likely be quashed by Congress; as Representative Christopher Shays said, nearly a year into the war on terror, "We're at war, and I'm saying I'm not going to look military personnel in the eye and say I voted against their budget." That's understandable, but it helps explain why we have a defense budget that is over half a trillion dollars, forty per cent higher than it was in 2001. More than half the federal government's discretionary spending goes to the military, and, while a sizable chunk goes toward the fight against terrorism and the Iraq war, too much has nothing to do with the demands of a post-9/11 world.

Over the past five years, we've heard a lot about the rise of what [former Secretary of Defense] Donald Rumsfeld likes to call "asymmetric warfare," and about the need to equip our military to fight "nontraditional" enemies. But a look at the defense budget shows that we're building a new military while still paying for the old one. Money is going into Special Operations and intelligence, but far more is being spent on high-tech weapons systems designed to fight enemies (like the Soviet Union) that no longer exist—eighty billion dollars on attack submarines, three billion apiece on new destroyers, and hundreds of billions on two different new models of jet fighter. Advocates insist that we need to be able to contest any "near peer" rival. But the U.S. has no near-peers—or, indeed, any distant peers, as we now spend more on defense than the rest of the world put together.

Stop Military Waste

Current plans call for us not only to spend hundreds of billions more in Iraq but to continue to spend even more over the next few years producing new weapons that might have been useful against the Soviet Union. Many of these weapons are technological marvels, but they have a central flaw: no conceivable enemy. It ought to be a requirement in spending all this money for a weapon that there be some need for it. In some cases we are developing weapons ... that lack not only a current military need but even a plausible use in any foreseeable future.

Barney Frank, "Cut the Military Budget—II,"
The Nation, *March 2, 2009.*

Irresponsible Spending

Not only are we buying stuff we don't need; we're buying it badly. Astonishing budget overruns are routine. The Future Combat System, for instance—designed to remake the battlefield with robot vehicles and networked communications systems—began as a ninety-billion-dollar project, then became a hundred-and-sixty-billion-dollar project, and, a recent Pentagon estimate suggests, will eventually cost three hundred billion dollars. Such inefficiency is seldom punished—the Pentagon often hands out bonuses even when companies fail to meet their targets—and is tolerated by regulators. Although government agencies have been required to produce an annual audit of their operations since the late nineties, the Defense Department's operations are so confused that it has never been able to produce a successful audit. A few years ago, the Pentagon's own Inspector General found that more than a trillion dollars in spending simply couldn't be explained.

Of course, people have been decrying Pentagon waste and inefficiency for decades. But things have got significantly worse over the past five years, because Congress and the [George W.] Bush Administration have thrown so much money at the Defense Department so fast. Studies of corporate behavior show that when companies are flush with cash they are more likely to make acquisitions that reduce their overall value. The defense industry today, in fact, is much like Silicon Valley in the late nineties—when you give lots of money to an industry with no audits and no supervision, people lose discipline. They spend on bad ideas, gild every surface, and cheat. Is it really a surprise that billions of dollars meant for private contractors in Iraq seems to have been stolen?

"The Mother of All Scoops"

The Defense Department is only asking for what it thinks it needs. But what it thinks it needs is determined in part by what it thinks it can get. A useful, if homely, analogy might be found in an experiment a group of social scientists did in an apartment building. One day, they left out a bowl of M&M's for people to take, with a small scoop beside it. When, the next day, they left a much larger scoop, people took two-thirds more M&M's. People could have taken just as many M&M's on the first day; they just would have had to take more scoops. They took more the second day because the larger scoop sent a message that that was what they were supposed to do. Congress and the President have, in effect, handed the Pentagon the mother of all scoops.

The fiscal consequences of this are obviously dismal, but, even worse, there's a strong possibility that giving the military a blank check is actually making us less safe. To begin with, although the defense budget is immense, it's not infinite. And often in recent times expensive weapons projects have been given priority over mundane improvements that would help the military here and now. Earlier this year, for instance, the

Senate cut funding for night-vision goggles for soldiers, while adding money to buy three new V-22 Ospreys, a plane that Dick Cheney himself tried to get rid of when he was Secretary of Defense. Similarly, we might have been able to afford appropriate body armor for the troops, and plates for the Hummers in Baghdad, if we were building only one new model of multi-billion-dollar jet fighter, instead of two.

Underfunding Crucial Programs

Even more strikingly, while we pour money into all these new projects we're underfunding crucial homeland-security programs. In the past few months, Congress has eliminated six hundred and fifty million dollars for port security. Funding for New York City's security projects was cut forty per cent. And we cut nearly a hundred million from the requested budget for preventing the use of nuclear weapons in the U.S. Those cuts were considered necessary for budgetary reasons, yet the price of all of them together was less than a third of what it will cost to build a single destroyer. That ship will offer us not a whit of protection in the war on terror. But we can be sure it will keep the seas safe from the Soviet Navy.

"*The economic consequences of Iraq run even deeper than the squandered opportunities for vital public investments. Spending on Iraq is also a job killer.*"

Too Much of the Federal Budget Has Gone to the Iraq War

Robert Pollin and Heidi Garrett-Peltier

Robert Pollin is a professor of economics and co-director of the Political Economy Research Institute (PERI) at the University of Massachusetts. Heidi Garrett-Peltier is a research assistant at PERI. In the following viewpoint, the authors argue that the Iraq War has been economically, as well as politically, disastrous. The money spent on the war is money not invested in public infrastructure—thus, costing the U.S. about one million jobs. While militarism does create jobs, investment in public infrastructure creates well-paid, domestic jobs more efficiently. With the country facing a recession, the authors argue that the government should expand public investment, creating more U.S. jobs.

Robert Pollin and Heidi Garrett-Peltier, "The Wages of Peace," *The Nation*, March 13, 2008. Copyright © 2008 by The Nation Magazine/The Nation Company, Inc. Reproduced by permission.

As you read, consider the following questions:

1. Why do the authors believe that sending rebate checks to taxpayers will not effectively stimulate the U.S. economy?

2. According to the authors, what three factors determine the overall job effects of a government program?

3. What do the authors predict would be the economic effects of transferring the 2007 Iraq War budget into public investments such as health care and education?

There is no longer any doubt that the Iraq War is a moral and strategic disaster for the United States. But what has not yet been fully recognized is that it has also been an economic disaster. To date, the government has spent more than $522 billion on the war, with another $70 billion already allocated for 2008.

With just the amount of the Iraq budget of 2007, $138 billion, the government could instead have provided Medicaid-level health insurance for all 45 million Americans who are uninsured. What's more, we could have added 30,000 elementary and secondary schoolteachers and built 400 schools in which they could teach. And we could have provided basic home weatherization for about 1.6 million existing homes, reducing energy consumption in these homes by 30 percent.

But the economic consequences of Iraq run even deeper than the squandered opportunities for vital public investments. Spending on Iraq is also a job killer. Every $1 billion spent on a combination of education, health care, energy conservation and infrastructure investments creates between 50 and 100 percent more jobs than the same money going to Iraq. Taking the 2007 Iraq budget of $138 billion, this means that upward of 1 million jobs were lost because the [George W.] Bush administration chose the Iraq sinkhole over public investment.

Recognizing these costs of the Iraq War is even more crucial now that the economy is facing recession. While a recession is probably unavoidable, its length and severity will depend on the effectiveness of the government's stimulus initiatives. By a wide margin, the most effective stimulus is to expand public investment projects, especially at the state and local levels. The least effective fiscal stimulus is the one crafted by the Bush administration and Congress—mostly to just send out rebate checks to all taxpayers. This is because a high proportion of the new spending encouraged by the rebates will purchase imports rather than financing new jobs in the United States, whereas public investment would concentrate job expansion within the country. Combining this Bush stimulus initiative with the ongoing spending on Iraq will only deepen the severity of the recession.

Is Militarism Necessary for Prosperity?

The government spent an estimated $572 billion on the military in 2007. This amounts to about $1,800 for every resident of the country. That's more than the combined GDPs [gross domestic products] of Sweden and Thailand, and eight times federal spending on education.

The level of military spending has risen dramatically since 2001, with the increases beginning even before 9/11. As a share of GDP, the military budget rose from 3 percent to 4.4 percent during the first seven years of the Bush presidency. At the current size of the economy, a difference between a military budget at 4.4 rather than 3 percent of GDP amounts to $134 billion.

The largest increases in the military budget during the Bush presidency have been associated with the Iraq War. Indeed, the $138 billion spent on Iraq in 2007 was basically equal to the total increase in military spending that caused the military budget to rise to 4.4 percent of GDP. It is often argued that the military budget is a cornerstone of the economy—that the Pentagon is a major underwriter of important technical innovations as well as a source of millions of decent jobs. At one level these claims are true. When the government spends upward of $600 billion per year of taxpayers' money on anything, it cannot help but generate millions of jobs. Similarly, when it spends a large share of that budget on maintaining and strengthening the most powerful military force in the history of the world, this cannot fail to encourage technical innovations that are somehow connected to the instruments of warfare.

A More Efficient Means of Job Creation

Yet it is also true that channeling hundreds of billions of dollars into areas such as renewable energy and mass transportation would create a hothouse environment supporting new technologies. For example, utilities in Arizona and Nevada are developing plans to build "concentrated" solar power plants, which use the sun to heat a liquid that can drive a turbine. It is estimated that this technology, operating on a large scale, could drive down the costs of solar electricity dramatically, from its current level of about $4 per watt to between $2.50 and $3 per watt in the sunniest regions of the country. At these prices, solar electricity becomes much cheaper than oil-driven power and within range of coal. These and related technologies could advance much more rapidly toward cost competitiveness with coal, oil and nuclear power if they were to receive even a fraction of the subsidies that now support weapons development (as well as the oil industry).

How does it happen that government spending devoted to health care, education, environmental sustainability and infrastructure can generate up to twice as many jobs per dollar as spending on militarism?

Three factors play a role in determining the overall job effects of any target of government spending. Let's compare the construction of Camp Victory, the main US military base on the western outskirts of Baghdad, with weatherizing existing homes in New England to increase their energy efficiency. The first factor to consider is the jobs that get created directly by each project. The second is the job creation in the industries that supply products for building the camp or weatherizing the homes. These would include the steel, concrete, weapons and telecommunications industries for building Camp Victory; and lumber, insulation and trucking industries for home weatherization. Finally, new jobs will result when people who are paid to build Camp Victory or weatherize a house spend the money they have earned—a weapons engineer at Camp Victory buying a lawnmower during his vacation leave at home or a construction worker in New England buying a new car.

Three Factors

How does one spending target create more jobs for a given amount of dollars spent? Still considering Camp Victory construction versus New England home weatherization, there are, again, three factors:

1. *More jobs but lower-paying jobs.* Average pay is lower in the construction industry working on home weatherization in New England than in mounting weapons installations at Camp Victory. So a given pool of money is divided among more employed people.

2. *More spending on people, less on machines and supplies.* In weatherizing a home, the machinery and supplies costs are relatively low, while the need for construction workers is high. Building a high-tech military base in Baghdad entails enormous investments in steel and sophisticated electronic equipment and relatively less spending for people on the job.

3. *More money stays within the US economy.* We roughly estimate that US military personnel spend only 43 percent of their income on domestic goods and services, while the overall population spends an average of 83 percent of their income on domestic products and 17 percent on imports.

It is important to know which of these three factors is relatively more important in generating the overall increase in jobs. In particular, it would not necessarily be a favorable development if the overall increase in employment opportunities is mainly just a byproduct of creating lots of low-paying jobs.

More Jobs or Better Jobs?

In fact, if we were simply to send a rebate to taxpayers for the full amount of the Iraq War budget—i.e., a measure similar to Bush's current stimulus plan—the increased spending on personal consumption would produce lots of what are now bad jobs, in areas such as retail, hotels, restaurants and personal services. Because of this, a transfer of funds from the military to tax rebates and personal consumption increases would produce a 25 percent increase in employment but an 11 percent decline in overall wages and benefits paid to working people.

The opposite is true with education as the spending target. Here, both the total number of jobs created and the average pay are higher than with the military. It's less clear-cut when it comes to health care, energy conservation and infrastructure investments. More jobs will be created than with military spending, and the total amount of wages and benefits going to workers will also be significantly higher than with military spending. But the average pay for a health care worker or those engaged in mass transit or construction is lower than in the military.

Is it better for overall economic welfare to generate more jobs, even if average wages and benefits are lower? There isn't a single correct answer to this question. It depends on the size of these differences: how many low-paying jobs are being generated, and how bad are these jobs? How many high-quality jobs would be sacrificed through a transition out of the military, where the average pay is relatively high? Indeed, by completely shutting off Iraq War–related spending and transferring the money in equal shares to education, health care, energy conservation and infrastructure, average salaries would decline. However, the majority of new jobs created by these peaceful alternatives would command salaries above a reasonable living-wage standard of $16 an hour.

Pushing Unemployment Down

As of January [2008] there were 7.6 million people unemployed in a labor force of 154 million, producing an official unemployment rate of 4.9 percent. This was a significant increase over the 4.5 percent unemployment rate in mid-2007, and thus one important sign of a weakening economy. Unemployment is likely to keep rising as the economic slowdown continues.

In our current context, what would be the overall job effects of transferring the entire 2007 Iraq War budget of $138 billion into health care, education, energy conservation and infrastructure investments? If we assume that all else would remain equal in the labor market, a net increase (i.e., the total expansion of jobs in public investments minus the reduction in military jobs) in the range of 1 million jobs would therefore reduce the total number of unemployed people to around 6.6 million. The unemployment rate would fall to about 4.3 percent.

This is still an unacceptably high unemployment rate. But if the public-investment-directed spending shift out of Iraq were combined with a stimulus package of roughly the same size as the Iraq War budget—i.e., in the range of the Bush administration's $150 billion stimulus—the overall impact would be a strong program to fight recession and create decent jobs.

In particular, through this combination of a spending shift out of Iraq and a stimulus program focused on public investment, there is a good chance that unemployment would fall below 4 percent. When unemployment fell below 4 percent in the late 1960s and late 1990s, the high demand for workers led to rising wages and benefits, in particular at the low end of the job market. Poverty fell as a result. Near full employment in the late '60s also brought better working conditions and less job discrimination against minorities.

Real Concerns

Of course, we cannot assume that everything about the labor market would stay unchanged after a huge job expansion in health care, education, energy conservation and infrastructure investments, while jobs connected with the military contracted. There would no doubt be skill shortages in some areas and labor gluts in others. There would also probably be an increase in inflation that would have to be managed carefully.

These concerns are real. But it is still true that large-scale job creation within the United States is possible as an outgrowth of ending the Iraq War, reallocating the entire Iraq budget to important domestic public investment projects and fighting the recession with further increases in public investments.

What if the Iraq War budget is transferred only partially to domestic public investments? Let's assume, optimistically, that a new administration takes serious initiatives to end the Iraq War immediately after coming into office next January. This new administration would almost certainly not have the wherewithal to shut down operations within one year. And even if it could completely end the war within a year, the government should still commit significant funds to war reparations for the Iraqi people.

Even a Partial Transfer of Funds Would Be Beneficial

The job expansion within the United States will decline to the extent that spending of any sort continues in Iraq rather than being transferred into domestic public investments. But even if the net transfer of funds is, say, $100 billion rather than $138 billion, several hundred thousand new domestic jobs would still be created. There is also no reason that the domestic public investment expansion has to mirror the decrease in the Iraq War budget. Any stimulus program initiated over the next few months—either a Bush-style program or one focused on public investment—would entail spending beyond the current Iraq budget levels.

There's also a strong argument for a stimulus program that emphasizes public investment at the state and local level. State and local government revenues—which primarily finance education, health care, public safety and infrastructure—are always badly hit by economic downturns and will be especially strapped as a result of the current recession. State and local government revenues decline when the incomes and property values of their residents fall. Property tax revenues will fall especially sharply as a result of the collapse of housing prices. Moreover, state and local governments, unlike the federal government, cannot run deficits and are forced to maintain balanced budgets, even in a recession. This means that unless the federal government injects new revenue into the state and local budgets, spending on public investments will decline.

Deficit Reduction: The Responsible Alternative?

The federal fiscal deficit in 2007 was $244 billion. Shutting down the Iraq War and using the fiscal savings to cut the deficit would mean a 57 percent deficit reduction.

Is this the best use of the funds released by the Iraq War? Of course, the government cannot run a reckless fiscal policy, no matter how pressing the country's social and environmental needs. But a $244 billion deficit in today's economy is not reckless. It amounts to about 1.8 percent of GDP. This is slightly below the average-sized deficit between 1960 and 2006 of 1.9 percent of GDP. The largest deviation from this long-term average occurred under Ronald Reagan's presidency, when the deficit averaged 4.2 percent of GDP—i.e., more than twice as large as the current deficit as a share of the economy.

The recession and stimulus program will of course produce a large increase in the deficit. Recessions are not the time to focus on deficit reduction. But even if we allowed the deficit to double from its 2007 level—to about $500 billion—its size, as a share of GDP, would still be below the average figure for the entire Reagan presidency, including both the boom and recession years.

How Money Is Spent Is the Issue

We would certainly need to worry about the deficit today, and even more after the recession ends, if it were persistently running at Reagan-era levels. This is because the government would soon be consuming upward of 20 percent of the total federal budget in interest payments, as it did at the end of the Reagan era. This is opposed to the 10 percent of total government spending we now pay to the Japanese and Chinese bondholders, US banks and wealthy private citizens who own the bulk of US government debt. But because the deficit has been at a reasonable level coming into the recession, the primary problem with the Treasury's fiscal stance is not the size of the deficit per se but how the money is being spent—that we are using the money for Iraq and a private consumption-led stimulus rather than public investment.

There are many good reasons government policy should now initiate major commitments to investment in the areas of health care, education, environmental sustainability and infra-structure. All these spending areas stand on their own merits. But moving the $138 billion spent on the Iraq War in 2007 into public investments will also increase employment, adding up to 1 million jobs. On top of this, expanding public invest-ment spending is the single most effective tool for fighting the recession.

A great deal is at stake here. The Iraq War has been about death and destruction. Ending the war could be a first serious step toward advancing a viable program for jobs, health care, education and a clean-energy economy.

"The biggest source of red ink in the federal budget is health care. And if we don't do anything about it, it will continue to be."

Too Much of the Federal Budget Is Spent on Health Care

George Krumbhaar

In the following viewpoint, George Krumbhaar asserts that the biggest single drain on the federal budget is health care costs. This is true for three main reasons: Health care has become more expensive, elderly Americans now account for more of the population than in the past, and political demand for health care spending has become seemingly limitless. At the same time, studies show a weak correlation between a nation's health care spending and health outcomes. Krumbhaar contends that a change to the health care system is needed before current costs bust the federal budget entirely. George Krumbhaar writes the "BudgetNow" column for CongressNow.

George Krumbhaar, "Health Care Costs Are Busting the Budget," *CongressNow*, July 20, 2007, p. Health. Copyright 2009. All rights reserved. Reprinted with permission from Roll Call/CongressNow.

As you read, consider the following questions:

1. According to Krumbhaar, how much has the proportion of the federal budget spent on Medicare and Medicaid grown since 1966?

2. What percentage of the American population is projected to be 65 or older in 2050?

3. How are federal discretionary health programs such as the National Institutes of Health paid for, according to Krumbhaar?

Forget Social Security, Iraq, even pork [earmarks, or "pet" projects]. The biggest source of red ink in the federal budget is health care. And if we don't do anything about it, it will continue to be.

Consider these health care budget facts:

- In 1966, Medicare and Medicaid took up 1 percent of the federal budget. By 1986, that share had increased to 10 percent. It now stands at 19 percent.

- At current rates of growth, federal spending on health care in 2050 will equal the share of the economy currently taken up by the entire federal budget. If we want to keep federal spending at its present level relative to the economy, there would be no room for any other programs—not defense, not education, not the environment.

- Despite this, the current health care system still leaves serious gaps in coverage. About 45 million Americans lack health insurance. If political leaders want to fill these gaps through expanding federal health care programs—as they did with the passage of prescription drug legislation in 2003—federal health care costs will escalate further.

The Federal Budget and Health Care Spending

The federal budget is on an unsustainable path, primarily because of rapidly rising spending on health care. Federal outlays for Medicare and Medicaid have increased from 1 percent of gross domestic product (GDP) in 1970 to more than 5 percent in 2009; and the Congressional Budget Office (CBO) projects that under current policy, they will exceed 6 percent of GDP in 2019 and about 8 percent in 2029. Most of that increase will result from rising costs per capita, rather than from the aging of the population. As a result, the country faces difficult and fundamental trade-offs between limiting the growth of Medicare and Medicaid relative to GDP, accepting a continuing increase in taxes relative to GDP, and reducing other spending relative to GDP, possibly to levels not experienced in this country in more than 40 years.

Congressional Budget Office,
"Health Care Reform and the Federal Budget," June 16, 2009.

And these figures represent only half of the problem. Private spending for health care equals public sector spending, and it has also been rising faster than the economy as a whole. There's political pressure to "reform" the health care system by making the federal government assume more of these private-sector costs.

Sources of the Problem

The sources of the health care dilemma are largely threefold:

First, as modern medicine gets more sophisticated, it gets more expensive. In fact, for several decades, health care costs have been rising faster than the consumer price index and faster than the growth rate of gross domestic product. If we do nothing, health care costs threaten to take over the economy.

Second, the aging of the population has put—and will continue to put—extra costs on the health care system and on federal health spending. Americans 65 and older now account for 12.5 percent of the population, up from 5 percent in 1900 and less than the 21 percent projected for 2050. Older Americans are sicker, and they consume more of the nation's health care bill.

In addition, Medicare and Medicaid carry a disproportionate burden of the elderly's health care costs. Congressional Budget Office testimony before the Senate Budget Committee revealed that Medicaid is the "largest single source of financing for long-term care in America today."

Third, demand for health care spending is, politically at least, almost boundless. It's difficult for a politician to declare that the United States should, as a matter of policy, limit the best health care only to the very wealthy.

Billions in Mandatory Health Programs Alone

How many dollars are at stake? Medicare, which stood at $31.0 billion in 1980, stands at $367.5 billion for the current fiscal year [2007], and the 2012 estimate is $481.6 billion. The corresponding figures for other mandatory health care programs, including Medicaid, are $14.7 billion for 1980, $214.9 billion for FY [fiscal year] 2007 and $225.1 billion in 2012. This does not include such federal discretionary health programs as veterans' medical care, the Indian Health Service and the National Institutes of Health. The latter programs are covered by annual appropriations. The former programs, Medicare and Medicaid included, are mandatory programs, meaning that any person who fits the eligibility standards is automatically entitled to the programs' benefits.

The $582.4 billion that Washington is spending on mandatory health programs compares with $581.9 billion we're spending on Social Security. That's virtually the same amount, but the mandatory health outlays have been growing since 1980 at more than 9 percent per year, compared with just over 6 percent for Social Security. According to the Government Accountability Office [GAO], the cost of the prescription drug program alone exceeds the total unfunded obligations for Social Security.

Theoretically, the solutions to rising federal health care costs are straightforward. They include a more holistic approach to health care, better criminal enforcement, stricter interpretation of existing rules and even a tightening of some eligibility standards.

Find a Solution, Create a Consensus

We are intrigued, however, with data from the Agency for Healthcare Research and Quality and the Center for Medicaid and Medicare Services. It was found that, within limits, there is only a weak relationship between per capita spending on Medicare and the quality of medical care for beneficiaries. The data compare quality outcomes against per capita costs that vary widely from region to region. This suggests that creative solutions exist out there short of cutting benefits. Indeed, many other countries can document better health care outcomes, at lower per capita costs, than the United States can.

Changing the present system will be difficult. Experience with the Medicare prescription drug benefit, which Congress passed, and President [George W.] Bush's privatization proposal for health care coverage, which fell by the wayside, tells us that it's easier to change federal health care policy through an expansion of coverage and costs rather than by attempts at economizing. Those who take the approach that we can cut health care costs by spending more wisely, however, have their work cut out for them. They need to create a consensus, which is so far missing.

The bottom line: As a GAO report in January [2007] plainly stated, "federal fiscal policy remains unsustainable." This is the case even though the budget may show a surplus from time to time over the near term. Although Social Security costs amid the retirement of the baby boomer generation have been getting a lot of headlines—and they are indeed a problem—the health costs of the same boomers and other Americans are the larger issue. Though most folks don't know this yet, a busted federal budget will be worse for their health than what they're getting now.

"*Our task . . . is to offer a new vision of a free society. . . . When that is accomplished the size and cost of government, over time, will be reduced accordingly.*"

Too Much of the Federal Budget Is Spent on Entitlements and Other Social Welfare Programs

Richard M. Ebeling

In the viewpoint below, Richard M. Ebeling, president of the Foundation for Economic Education, argues that the 2008 federal budget reflects the federal government's misplaced priorities. Instead of debating how much the government should fund social programs, lawmakers should be deciding whether they should fund them at all. Ebeling decries the modern welfare state, which spends, for example, 52.6 percent of the budget on "entitlement" programs, such as Social Security and Medicare. He calls for a return to smaller government, with priorities limited by the primary functions of government laid out by the Constitution: securing citizens' rights to life, liberty, and property.

Richard M. Ebeling, "The Cost of the Federal Government in a Freer America," *The Freeman: Ideas on Liberty*, vol. 57, March 2007. Copyright 2007 Foundation for Economic Education, Incorporated, www.thefreemanonline.org. All rights reserved. Reproduced by permission.

As you read, consider the following questions:

1. According to Ebeling, how much money does the average American household pay toward the federal budget?

2. What were the seven executive departments in the 1868 federal government?

3. What inspired the growth of the U.S. federal government, according to Ebeling?

In February [2007], President George W. Bush submitted his proposed federal budget for the fiscal year [2008] that begins in October. It called for total government spending of over $2.9 trillion. The administration and the Republicans in Congress insisted that this budget reflected fiscal responsibility and the promise of a return to a balanced budget a few years down the road. The Democrats, on the other hand, declared the budget "dead on arrival" because it set the wrong priorities and was too harsh to the "neediest" in society.

What the two major political parties and the administration are debating is how much should be spent and on what. What none of them ask, or even seem to consider, is whether the federal government should be spending taxpayers' money on the vast majority of these programs and activities.

The late Senator Everett Dirksen is purported to have once quipped in the 1960s, "A billion here, a billion there, pretty soon you're talking about real money." In President Bush's budget it is the hundreds of billions to be spent here and there that add up to the real money. If we break down the President's budget we find the following planned expenditures: $919.1 billion on Medicare and Medicaid; $607.7 billion on Social Security; $510.8 billion on other nondefense spending; $602.9 billion on defense expenditures; and $261.3 billion on net interest owed on the national debt.

"Entitlement" spending (Medicare, Medicaid, and Social Security) would absorb 52.6 percent of the budget; other nondefense spending would consume 17.6 percent; defense spending would take 20.8 percent; and interest payments on the federal debt would be 9 percent.

Beyond "Out of Control"

Among cabinet-level departments there would be the following increases in spending: Veterans Affairs, 13.3 percent; State, 12.9 percent; Health and Human Services, 8.7 percent; Labor, 7.9 percent; Housing and Urban Development, 7.1 percent; Treasury, 6.9 percent; Energy, 5.4 percent; Defense, 4.1 percent; Agriculture, 3.6 percent; and Transportation, 2.7 percent. These increases are all above the current rate of increase in the Consumer Price Index.

The administration estimates that total federal revenues from all taxing sources would be $2.662 trillion. The deficit for the fiscal year, therefore, would come to $239 billion, or about 8.2 percent of expenditures.

It is estimated that $1.247 trillion dollars would be collected in individual income taxes; $927.2 billion would come from Social Security, Medicare, and related receipts; $314.5 billion would be obtained from corporate income taxes, $68.1 billion from excise taxes, $25.7 billion from estate and gift taxes, $29.2 billion from customs duties and fees, and $50.6 billion from "miscellaneous" sources of tax revenue.

With a U.S. population of about 301,150,000, a federal budget of $2.901 trillion means a per capita federal burden on every man, woman, and child of about $9,634. With an estimated 112,250,000 American households, this means each household would bear a burden, on average, of $25,845. (This does not count the burden of state and local taxes.)

Some of the more "strict constructionist" conservatives in Congress occasionally say the federal government is "out of control" and far beyond the "original intent" of the Constitution. But virtually none challenges what the federal government does, nor do they propose abolishing those departments, bureaus, agencies, and activities that clearly are not "strictly" enumerated in the Constitution.

And most certainly no one in the halls of power asks the fundamental question: What should be the functions of government if its only purpose is understood to be securing each individual's right to life, liberty, and property?

The Original Intent of the Budget

According to the 1868 World Almanac (the first year it was published), the responsibilities of the federal government were far fewer than today, even in the aftermath of the Civil War. There were only seven executive departments: Treasury, State, War, Navy, Interior, Attorney General, and Postmaster General.

Let's suppose the federal government's responsibilities today were only as extensive as they were in 1868. And just for the sake of argument, let's suppose each of these departments and branches of government [cost only] half of what President [George W.] Bush proposes, since the federal arm of government would be far less intrusive in people's lives. What would be the cost of government and the tax burden on the American citizenry?

Making the roughest of estimates from the President's budget, the federal government would cost only about $622 billion. (This includes the $262.3 billion in net interest payments on the federal debt. If this debt did not exist, the hypothetical budget would be around $360 billion.)

Again roughly speaking, the imagined budget would mean a tax burden of only $2,065 per capita. And the average tax imposed on households would be about $5,540. In other words, the burden would be almost 80 percent less than what President Bush wants. Also, this would assure a balanced budget in the coming fiscal year, not in some politically manipulated and uncertain future.

Shifting Priorites

Federal spending, 1956 and 2006

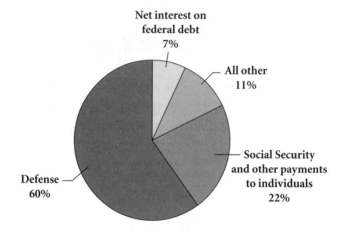

Net interest on
federal debt
7%

All other
11%

Social Security
and other payments
to individuals
22%

Defense
60%

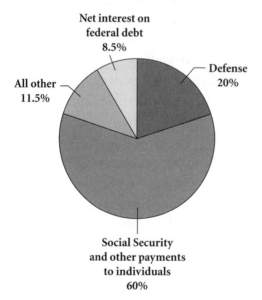

Net interest on
federal debt
8.5%

Defense
20%

All other
11.5%

Social Security
and other payments
to individuals
60%

Original Source: Office of Management and Budget

TAKEN FROM: Robert Samuelson, "The Stubborn Welfare State," *Real Clear Politics*, February 14, 2007.

What makes the real difference between this imagined budget and the one actually submitted? Of course, the welfare state! All the departments, bureaus, and agencies that have been added to the federal government since those far more laissez-faire days of the mid-nineteenth century have been the product of the interventionist and redistributive state.

Laughlin's Wisdom

In 1887 J. Laurence Laughlin, who founded the economics department at the University of Chicago, warned:

> Socialism, or the reliance on the state for help, stands in antagonism to self-help, or the activity of the individual. That body of people is certainly the strongest and the happiest in which each person is thinking for himself, is independent, self-respecting, self-confident, self-controlled, and self-mastered. When a man does a thing for himself he values it infinitely more than if it is done for him, and he is a better man for having done it. . . . If, on the other hand, men constantly hear it said that they are oppressed and downtrodden, deprived of their own, ground down by the rich, and that the state will set all things right for them in time, what other effect can that teaching have on the character and energy of the ignorant than the complete destruction of all self-help? They think that they can have commodities which they have not helped to produce. They begin to believe that two and two make five. . . . The danger of enervating [weakening] results flowing from dependence on the state for help should cause us to restrict the interference of legislation as far as is possible, and should be permitted only when there is an absolute necessity, and even then it should be undertaken with hesitation.

Laughlin added, "The right policy is a matter of supreme importance, and we should not like to see in our country the system of interference as exhibited in the paternal theory of government existing in France and Germany."

The Welfare State Continues Out of Inertia

Unfortunately, America did import the theory and policy of political paternalism from the collectivist trends then growing stronger in Europe. They became the basis and rationale for a far bigger government in the United States beginning in the Progressive Era in the early decades of the twentieth century and accelerating in the New Deal days of the Roosevelt administration in the 1930s. They have continued ever since under both Democrats and Republicans.

But the ideological wind is out of the sails of the interventionist welfare state. It continues to exist in America and indeed around the world not because most people really believe that government can solve all their ills and make a paradise on earth, but out of pure political inertia. Our task, however daunting it may seem at times, is to offer a new vision of a free society that can once again capture the excitement and confidence of our fellow citizens. When that is accomplished the size and cost of government, over time, will be reduced accordingly.

> *"Not only are all other entitlements growing considerably more slowly than the 'big three,' but they are actually projected to shrink as a share of the economy through 2050."*

Spending on Some Entitlement Programs Is Actually Decreasing

Aviva Aron-Dine and Robert Greenstein

Aviva Aron-Dine worked as a policy analyst at the Center on Budget and Policy Priorities (CBPP) from 2005 to 2008. Robert Greenstein is the CBPP's founder and executive director. In the following viewpoint, Aron-Dine and Greenstein dispute the argument that there is a general "entitlement crisis" as a result of increased expenditures on entitlements, those benefits guaranteed by law. In fact, they say, spending has risen only on the "big three" entitlements—Medicare, Medicaid, and Social Security. Spending on other entitlement programs has actually slowed in recent years, and is projected to shrink as a share of the economy through 2050.

As you read, consider the following questions:

1. According to the authors, why will it be nearly impossible to keep the rate of growth in health cares costs below the rate of growth of the gross domestic product (GDP) in the future?

2. How much will the "big three" entitlement programs grow between 2007 and 2017 after adjusting for inflation and population growth, according to projections by the Congressional Budget Office (CBO)?

3. Why will the cost of entitlement programs other than the "big three" decline as a share of the economy, according to the authors?

As is well known, the United States will face grave budget challenges in coming decades. In a new set of federal budget projections through 2050, we find that if current policies remain unchanged, federal expenditures will increase substantially as a share of the economy and revenues will fall short of covering expenditures by increasing amounts, leading to exploding deficits and debt. Long-term budget projections by other institutions and analysts reach the same conclusion.

The primary sources of the projected expenditure growth are demographic changes (the aging of the population) and rapidly rising health care costs. Together, these factors will cause Medicare, Medicaid, and Social Security obligations to grow considerably faster than the economy.

Many pundits and policymakers, however, have mistakenly described the projected rise in federal expenditures as an "entitlement crisis." That phrase is problematic, as it can mislead policymakers and the public into thinking that the source of expenditure growth is *most or all* entitlement programs, rather than just the "big three." It may even cause them to think that all entitlement programs, regardless of their design or purpose, necessarily grow unsustainably. (Some journalists have gone further and have actually asserted that entitlements other than the "big three" are contributing to the long-run fiscal problem. A recent *Wall Street Journal* editorial, for example, blamed growth in "Medicare, Medicaid, Social Security, food stamps, and the like" for the projected rise in federal expenditures.)

Other Programs Don't Contribute to Fiscal Problem

In fact, not only are all other entitlements growing considerably more slowly than the "big three," but they are actually projected to *shrink* as a share of the economy through 2050. . . . That is, if current policies in these programs are maintained, "other entitlements" will consume a *smaller* share of the nation's resources in 2050 than they do today.

Since these programs are growing more slowly than the economy, they are not contributors to the long-run fiscal problem. In the absence of legislative changes, revenues generally grow slightly faster than the economy. Program growth that is similar to or slower than GDP [gross domestic product] growth thus will also be similar to, or slower than, revenue growth. As a result, the other entitlement programs, which will grow more slowly than the economy, will grow more slowly than revenues as well. They [will thus] not contribute to the increasing mismatch between revenues and expenditures that is the cause of the mounting deficits and debt.

(This is not meant to imply that *no* program *should* grow faster than the economy. In particular, the rate of growth in Medicare and Medicaid costs per beneficiary is driven largely by the rate of growth in health-care costs system-wide, and it will likely prove impossible to reduce that rate of growth so markedly that these costs rise no faster than GDP. This is because the primary factor driving health care expenditures upward is advances in medical technology, which improve health and increase longevity but raise overall health care costs; it is inconceivable Americans will not want to avail themselves of such medical advances in the decades ahead. If, however, some programs *do* rise faster in cost than GDP, that growth will have to be paid for in some way. . . .)

The "Other Entitlements" Are Growing at Moderate and Sustainable Rates

That other entitlement programs (programs other than the "big three") are growing more slowly than GDP can be seen first by examining the Congressional Budget Office's detailed projections for these programs, which are available through 2017. . . . CBO projects that over the next ten years, the "big three" entitlement programs will grow 39 percent after adjusting for inflation and population growth, and by almost 2 percentage points as a share of GDP. In contrast, the "other entitlements" in total are projected to be essentially constant after adjusting for inflation and population growth and to *decline* modestly as a share of GDP. In addition, . . . nearly all individual "other entitlement" programs—for example, food stamps, refundable tax credits such as the Earned Income tax credit, and Temporary Assistance for Needy Families (TANF)—are projected to decline somewhat as a share of GDP.

Our projections also show that if current policies are maintained, "other entitlement" spending will continue to shrink as a share of GDP through 2050, simply due to the nature of these programs. Entitlement programs are, broadly speaking, structured so that as long as there are no changes in policy, they continue to provide an approximately constant level of services to a specified eligible population. (For example, if current policies are maintained, the Food Stamp Program will continue to provide an approximately constant benefit in food purchasing power to each individual who meets the program's income and other eligibility criteria.) Expenditures in entitlement programs generally increase at the rates necessary to continue to provide the same level of services to the eligible population.

An Imagined Crisis

Dwelling on an imagined "entitlement crisis" is triply misleading. It directs attention to pensions and other non-health programs that pose no serious budgetary challenge. It diverts attention from health care reform, the problem which—if addressed effectively—will remove the long-term fiscal challenge. And it suggests that the health care problem is just in the public sector, when the real challenge—and the only way to meet it—is to reform the whole health care system. That is the nation's long-term fiscal challenge.

Henry J. Aaron, "There Is No Entitlement Crisis,"
The Brookings Institution, *February 23, 2009.*

Growth in Spending Determined by Growth in Eligible Population

In the case of Medicare, Medicaid, and Social Security, providing the legislatively determined benefit package to the specified eligible population will entail rapid cost growth over coming decades. Because health care costs are projected to grow substantially faster than the economy, providing the same level of health services will result in Medicare and Medicaid expenditures rising faster than the economy. Moreover, since the size of the elderly population is projected to increase substantially, Medicare and Social Security (and, to a lesser degree, Medicaid) also will need to grow just to continue to serve all eligible individuals who apply.

By contrast, in the case of the other entitlement programs, maintaining current services for the eligible population will *not* require rapid expenditure growth. In general, it will simply require that expenditures keep pace with inflation and growth in the size of the U.S. population. And since the economy is projected to grow more quickly than inflation plus population growth, the cost of these other entitlement programs will continue declining as a share of the economy. This is not because these programs are being cut but rather because, as the nation grows richer, the same level of per-person services can be provided using a smaller share of the nation's resources.

Not Part of the "Crisis"

Of course, the "other entitlements" category includes a diverse group of programs, some of which will need to grow more quickly than inflation and population growth to maintain current services, and others of which will grow more slowly. In the aggregate, however, assuming that "other entitlements" will grow with inflation and population in the decades after 2017 is likely to be the best method of projecting the total cost of these programs. As noted, the Congressional Budget Office projects that over the next ten years, these programs will grow at rates virtually identical to the combined rate of inflation and population growth. Furthermore, the Congressional Research Service projects that civil service retirement and disability, the largest of the "other entitlements" programs, will grow more slowly than the rate of inflation plus population growth through 2050.

The other entitlement programs do not bear responsibility for the substantial rise in federal expenditures as a share of GDP that is projected under current policy. The growth rates of these programs under current law are moderate and fully sustainable. They should not be described as presenting or contributing to a "crisis."

Claiming there is a general entitlement crisis thus is not a useful simplification. Rather, it can leave policymakers with mistaken impressions about the nature and causes of our long-term fiscal difficulties and may lead them to inappropriate policies.

| "*Dramatic increases in resources have not led to improvement in the performance of our students.*"

Increased Spending Has Not Improved Education

Tom Bethell

In the following viewpoint, Tom Bethell argues that the expansion of the federal government's role in education since 1970 has not resulted in a better education system. Democrats and Republicans alike believe that the more budget money is spent on education, the more schools will improve. This has not been demonstrated to be true, Bethell says, citing numerous cases of school districts that saw little to no improvement in the quality of their schools after receiving vastly more funding. Tom Bethell is a senior editor of the American Spectator *and the author of* The Politically Incorrect Guide to Science.

As you read, consider the following questions:

1. Why did courts initially get involved in the school funding issue, according to Bethell?

Tom Bethell, "Spending More, Learning Less," *The American Spectator*, vol. 39, December 2006/January 2007, pp. 66–69. Copyright ©.The American Spectator 2007. Reproduced by permission.

2. What destroyed Washington, D.C.'s Dunbar High
   School's tradition of excellence, according to the authors
   of *Courting Failure?*

3. What does Bethell predict will be the fate of No Child
   Left Behind?

The U.S. Department of Education was created in 1979,
with an initial budget of about $15 billion. Within a few
months, on the campaign trail, Ronald Reagan was calling for
its abolition. He renewed that rallying cry in his first State of
the Union address. As late as 1996, the Republican Party was
still talking about abolishing the department, but by then everyone must have known it was too late. (Sen. Tom Coburn of
Oklahoma remains a valiant abolitionist to this day.)

Between 1970 and 2000, government spending on education, adjusted for inflation, rose from about $3,000 per pupil
to $5,600. Then came President [George W.] Bush's No Child
Left Behind law. More spending increases were on the way—
but dismayed conservatives were given a bone. With the money
would come "accountability": students would have to take
tests from time to time.

Having sent nearly all its political contributions to the
Democrats, and numerous delegates to the Democratic Con-
vention, the National Education Association [NEA] was happy.
And no doubt surprised. Bush, eager to show that his heart
was in the right place when it came to government schooling,
had joined forces with Ted Kennedy.

By 2004, Bush saw the expanded federal role in education
as an *accomplishment* of his presidency. If Republicans would
only spend more, he seemed to think, Democrats would have
no reason to accuse them of miserliness. Federal spending on
education received a bigger boost from 2002 to 2004 than in
all the eight years of the [President Bill] Clinton administration. Today [2007], the budget of the Department of Education is about $58 billion.

An Accepted Notion

All liberals and probably most conservatives accept that if more government money is spent to reach some goal, the nation will come closer to attaining it. More money for the Department of Education, for example, means that schoolchildren will get a better education. President Bush seems to have accepted that without a second thought.

In Washington, almost all the forces are arrayed on one side. The teacher unions and the education industry press for more money, and the people mostly still believe that more money will translate into better education. Legislators who vote for the increases have reason to expect that they will be rewarded with votes. The problem is that when the man who should resist these self-interested parties, the President of the United States, himself supports more spending, the taxpayers are the losers.

Now there's another and growing source of pressure: the judiciary. Courts first became involved because some school districts were spending more than others. That was judged unfair. Then came a new rationale for judicial intervention—"adequacy." In an Alabama district, where spending across school districts was equal, students were still doing poorly. Why? Because the funding was inadequate, lawyers argued. Judges happily accepted that.

But as Eric Hanushek argues in a new book, *Courting Failure*, "dramatic increases in resources have not led to improvement in the performance of our students." This fascinating collection of articles by a task force on education at the Hoover Institution makes the case that intervention by judges may actually have done more harm than good (to children; not necessarily to administrators). The book also raises basic questions about the effectiveness of government spending in this field.

"Accountability" Fails

The new emphasis on testing was intended to expose low-performing schools. Threatened with a loss of funds, they would surely have an incentive to do better. Nonetheless, "accountability" soon became a weapon in the hands of the "spend-more" crowd. In 2005, the NEA filed a lawsuit against the Department of Education, demanding that it pump up spending on poverty performing schools. Then they would have the "resources" to meet the new standards. Without argument, poor performance was attributed to an insufficiency of dollars. That was treated as a given.

Sol Stern, who writes on education issues for *City Journal*, has a good chapter in *Courting Failure* on recent developments in the New York schools. A judge has ruled that schools should receive an additional $5.63 billion a year, and soon enough the state's high court is expected to order the legislature to cough up the money.

The underlying theory—more money yields better schooling—received a real world test even as the case was litigated (over 13 years). In 1992, New York City spent an average of $7,495 per student. In the '90s this soared to almost $12,000 (or $12.5 billion total). Now, the overall budget is up to about $17 billion. Yet judges and New York pols [politicians] say they must have another $5.4 billion a year. Annual expenditures for the city's schools would then reach $22 billion, or about $20,000 per student.

Since the original lawsuit was filed in 1993, Stern writes, "total spending for the city's schools has more than doubled." Yet it hasn't affected the results. "More than half of the city's children still can't read at grade level, and only 15 percent of New York City students graduated with a Regents diploma." Stern calls this whole exercise a "March of Folly."

Kansas City Experiment

In a separate essay Williamson M. Evers and Paul Clopton examine other school districts that spend high and achieve low: among them Kansas City, Missouri; Washington, D.C.; and many districts in New Jersey.

From 1984 to 1997, Kansas City was subjected to a court experiment in lavish spending (ordered by Federal District Judge Russell Clark). It reached about $12,000 per student, more than double the state average. Almost half the state's education budget went to two districts with less than 10 percent of the state's students. Fifteen new schools were built, dozens more were renovated, and an Olympic-sized swimming pool was added for good measure.

A million-dollar advertising campaign tried to lure suburban students back to the city's schools. They could even come by taxi, the fare to be paid by the school district. Student-teacher ratios of 12 or 13 to 1 were the lowest of any major district in the country. To fund his experiment, Judge Clark, in disregard of all constitutional precedent, ordered a doubling of Kansas City's property tax rates.

Criminal mismanagement was just one outcome. "Employees stole hundreds of thousands of dollars worth of equipment every year, finance officers wrote checks directly to themselves, and insiders described the atmosphere as that of a 'third world country' suddenly endowed with 'unlimited wealth,'" the authors write.

Teacher salaries were raised 50 percent in one year, yet the quality of new hires was unaffected. As for the results, they were "as disappointing as the corruption, inefficiency and mismanagement. Test scores failed to improve over the course of the program." Kansas City remained 10 to 20 points below the state average. The black-white gap didn't go away, and by the mid-1990s few white students remained in the district. As a result, "nonwhite enrollment was above 90 percent in many schools."

The authors conclude that Kansas City's schools "may have been among the best funded in the country, but they remain among the worst performing to this day." In 2000 the district

Increased Funding Doesn't Mean Increased Performance

There's little reason to believe ... dramatic funding increases will lead to improvements in student learning in American schools. Since the early 1970s, inflation-adjusted federal spending per pupil has doubled. Over that period, student performance has not markedly improved, according to the long-term National Assessment of Educational Progress (NAEP), which is designed to measure historical trends.

"The Facts on Federal Education Spending,"
Education Notebook, *Heritage Foundation,*
November 9, 2006.

"flunked everyone of eleven performance measures for accreditation, which it lost." It has been kept going recently thanks to the Bill and Melinda Gates Foundation, which seems to enjoy giving more money to whatever the government has already lavishly funded.

D.C. Schools in Crisis

Washington, D.C.'s government schools tell a no less remarkable story. "All too few of the schoolchildren of the District of Columbia Public Schools can read, write and calculate," Evers and Clopton allow. "Its schools are in crisis, despite huge spending on public education." A control board appointed by President Clinton concluded that "for each additional year that students stay in the D.C. Public Schools, the less likely they are to succeed."

In 2003, D.C. eighth graders barely outscored U.S. fourth graders in math, and for the last 40 years almost half of its eighth grade students have failed to graduate. In College Board

SAT [Scholastic Aptitude Test] scores Washington's students score way below the rest of the country, "despite funding levels at 50 percent, 60 percent and even 70 percent above the national average."

Even as pupil enrollment declined by 33,000, the system's central office staff doubled. One administrator sufficed for 42 teachers across the nation, but there was one for every 16 in Washington, D.C. No one bothered with academics or student achievement. The tradition of excellence at Dunbar High School, from which many blacks graduated at an outstanding level in earlier decades, was destroyed after *Brown v. Board of Education* (1954) when it became a neighborhood school. Of this calamity the authors write:

> Enough of these neighborhood students were so highly disruptive and inadequately motivated that Dunbar's ethos of excellence was soon under siege. When district administrators and Washington, D.C. politicians declined to defend that ethos, Dunbar's all-star teaching staff retired or moved away, and its motto ("Perseverance is king") was replaced by self-serving excuses. Today, although Dunbar has better facilities and funding than it ever had during its eighty-five year reign as a jewel of student achievement, Dunbar is a failing ghetto school.

In his book *Black Rednecks and White Liberals* (2005), Thomas Sowell explores the almost willful destruction of Dunbar High School. One is left wondering whether liberals really are interested in black educational achievement. Perhaps they prefer black failure as a sign of the persistently unregenerate character of American society.

New Jersey Schools

When it comes to spending on government schooling, New Jersey is the most profligate in the nation. A class-action suit on behalf of students from poorer districts claimed that these students were both receiving less money and doing far worse academically than those from well-to-do districts. It was known as *Abbott v. Burke*. The court ordered the poorer (known as *Abbott*) districts to receive as much money per student as was being spent in the well-to-do districts.

In 1999, the state supreme court ordered up the following menu: "put into effect whole-school reform, provide full-day nursery school and kindergarten for all three- and four-year olds, launch a state-managed building program, provide advanced technology and additional vocational education, summer-school and after-school programs."

Today, New Jersey spends about $12,000 per student per year on average, but in some *Abbott* districts it is as high as $18,000. By comparison, suburban (non-*Abbott*) districts spend about $10,000 a year per student. What are the results? Despite an additional $3 billion spent on the schools, Evers and Clopton write,

> there has been no improvement across the *Abbott* districts. Student achievement in New Jersey's lowest-income school districts is persistently far worse than that in other school districts in the state. As Peter Denton—founder and chairman of Excellent Education for Everyone—says, the "horrible reality" is that over the several decades in which New Jersey has tripled spending on its low-income urban schools, their performance has "steadily declined" as measured by college attendance rates, standardized test scores, K-12 [kindergarten through high school] attendance rates, and high school graduation rates.

A Tenet Central to Liberalism

The authors also have excellent accounts of what has gone on (and gone wrong) in the Cambridge, Massachusetts district, graced by Harvard and MIT, which spends twice the state average per pupil, and Sausalito, California, one of the richest suburbs of San Francisco. Cambridge consistently performs below the state and even the national average for grade level reading and math; Sausalito actually receives $24,388 per student in funds, yet performance is dismal there, too. But there is no need to go on. You get the picture by now.

The belief that "dollars spent" is a reliable proxy for performance will not go away any time soon. It is central to the liberal faith as a whole, and it won't be abandoned without a huge fight. At the moment only libertarians seem capable of challenging the idea. Oxymoronic "big government conservatives" actively support it. And, alas, we have not even reached the stage where a *Republican* president can be expected to resist big spending on principle.

Educational testing has the merit of allowing the success of a few government programs to be measured. In most government fields, this is not so easy. So it comes as no surprise to read (in the *Washington Post* . . .) that "Political Backlash Builds Over High-Stakes Testing." A Democrat running for governor in Florida has decided that school tests are "punitive," But when students routinely fail them, one hopes that there is some penalty. That's what tests are for. As for the parents, they are said to be "outraged"; not because their kids are doing poorly in school, but because tests make such failure more conspicuous.

It's easy to predict the fate of No Child Left Behind. The spending increases will be pocketed and the "accountability" will be junked.

Periodical Bibliography

The following articles have been selected to supplement the diverse views presented in this chapter.

Fred Barnes   "Going on Offense for Missile Defense," *Weekly Standard*, August 7, 2006.

Jonathan Chait   "Hurry Up and Waste," *New Republic*, March 4, 2009.

Peter Ferrara   "The Public Policy," *New American*, September 2008.

Christopher Hayes   "Cut the Military Budget—II," *Nation*, March 2, 2009.

Adam J. Hebert   "Defense and the Economy," *Air Force Magazine*, May 2009.

Peter Barton Hutt   "Funding FDA: A Call for Action," *Food Technology*, September 2007.

Nation   "It's the War Economy, Stupid!" March 31, 2008.

Alex Newman   "Cancerous Growth of Government," *New American*, May 11, 2009.

Eric Pfeiffer   "The Budget-Cutters Who Couldn't Stop Spending," *Reason*, December 2006.

Robert J. Samuelson   "Obama's Unhealthy Choices," *Newsweek*, January 19, 2009.

Luiza Ch. Savage   "The Shockingly Liberal Legacy of George W. Bush," *Maclean's*, September 1, 2008.

Bruce Stokes   "Ending Farm Subsidies," *National Journal*, February 24, 2007.

Mark Thompson   "Taming the System," *Time*, February 23, 2009.

For Further Discussion

Chapter 1

1. After reading this chapter, do you agree with Jim Bates, that the federal budget process needs to be reformed? If so, which parts of the process do you feel need to be changed—and why?

2. Do you agree with Veronique de Rugy that the appropriations process is useful, but has been used wrongly—or do you find this process implicitly flawed?

Chapter 2

1. Now that you've read the contrary positions of the Concord Coalition and Alan Reynolds on the impact of federal budget deficits, what is your impression of the degree of harm they cause?

2. After reading all the viewpoints in this chapter, to what extent do you think cutting the federal deficit should determine fiscal policy?

Chapter 3

1. After reading the viewpoints by Robert L. Borosage and Celinda Lake and by J.T. Young, do you think wealthy Americans should take on more of the federal tax burden—or do they pay enough in taxes already?

2. How well do you think the sin taxes currently in place work, in terms of increasing budget revenue and deterring certain behaviors? What do you think of Nick Gillespie's proposal to expand sin taxes?

Chapter 4

1. Considering some of the figures cited by George Krumb-haar and Richard M. Ebeling, do you agree that the federal government spends too much money on entitlement programs like Medicaid, Medicare, and Social Security? If so, how should these programs be cut?

2. As a student, are you convinced by Tom Bethell's argument that increased federal spending on education has not improved education? Why or why not?

Organizations to Contact

The editors have compiled the following list of organizations concerned with the issues debated in this book. The descriptions are derived from materials provided by the organizations. All have publications or information available for interested readers. The list was compiled on the date of publication of the present volume; the information provided here may change. Be aware that many organizations take several weeks or longer to respond to inquiries, so allow as much time as possible.

American Enterprise Institute for Public Policy Research (AEI)
1150 Seventeenth Street NW, Washington, DC 20036
(202) 862-5800 • fax: (202) 862-7177
Web site: www.aei.org

The American Enterprise Institute for Public Policy Research is a private, nonpartisan research and education institution dedicated to the principles of democratic capitalism, limited government, individual liberty, and vigilant and effective defense and foreign policies. It sponsors research classified in three primary divisions: economic policy studies, social and political studies, and defense and foreign policy studies. Publications include a monthly newsletter, *The American* magazine, books such as *Tax Policy Lessons from the 2000s*, and papers and studies such as "The Deficit Endgame" and "Facts and Figures About Homeland Security Spending."

The Brookings Institution
1775 Massachusetts Ave. NW, Washington, DC 20036
(202) 797-6000
Web site: www.brookings.edu

The Brookings Institution is a public policy organization that emphasizes strengthening American democracy; supporting the economic and social welfare, security, and opportunity of all Americans; and securing a more open, safe, prosperous, and cooperative international system. The institution publishes various newsletters, including the *Economic Studies Bulletin* as well as journals such as *Brookings Papers on Economic Activity* and books such as *Using Taxes to Reform Health Insurance*.

The Cato Institute
1000 Massachusetts Ave. NW, Washington, DC   20001
(202) 842-0200 • fax: (202) 842-3490
Web site: www.cato.org

The Cato Institute is a public policy research foundation that promotes limited government, individual liberty, free markets, and peace. In addition to research, it provides educational information and encourages greater involvement of citizens in public policy discussions. The institute publishes the *Cato Journal, Cato Policy Report, Tax and Budget Bulletin*, the *Economic Development Bulletin*, and several other publications.

Center on Budget and Policy Priorities (CBPP)
820 First Street NE, Suite 510, Washington, DC   20002
(202) 408-1080 • fax: (202) 408-1056
e-mail: center@cbpp.org
Web site: www.cbpp.org

The Center on Budget and Policy Priorities is an organization concerned with the effects of budget and tax policy on low-income families and individuals. It conducts research and analysis to inform public debates about economic policy and develops policy options to eliminate poverty. The Center publishes *Policy Points*, as well as other reports, analyses, fact sheets, and policy statements.

The Club for Growth
2001 L Street, Suite 600, Washington, DC   20036
(202) 955-5500 • fax: (202) 955-9466
Web site: www.clubforgrowth.org

The Club for Growth is a network of citizens promoting economic freedom and growth. Its policy goals include death tax repeal, cuts in government spending, Social Security reform, expansion of free trade, and regulatory reform. The Club for Growth publishes an annual *Congressional Scorecard* and House and Senate *Repork Cards.*

Committee for a Responsible Federal Budget (CRFB)
1899 L Street NW, Suite 400, Washington, DC 20036
(202) 986-6599 • fax: (202) 986-3696
e-mail: crfb@newamerica.net
Web site: www.crfb.org

The Committee for a Responsible Federal Budget is a nonprofit organization dedicated to educating the public about fiscal policy and related issues. It runs the U.S. Budget Watch and Fiscal Roadmap projects, as well as the Peterson-Pew Commission on Budget Reform and others. The CRFB publishes periodic Budget Updates and Policy Papers, as well as other publications such as *Deficit Reduction: Lessons from Around the World* and *The Long-Term Budget Outlook.*

Concord Coalition
1011 Arlington Blvd., Suite 300, Arlington, VA 22209
(703) 894-6222 • fax: (703) 894-6231
e-mail: concordcoalition@concordcoalition.org
Web site: www.concordcoalition.org

The Concord Coalition is a nonpartisan organization that advocates for generationally responsible fiscal policy. It is committed to educating the public about the causes and consequences of federal budget deficits through lectures, classes, and media interviews across the country. The coalition's publications include *The Washington Budget Report, Facing Facts,* issue briefs, and more.

Congressional Budget Office (CBO)
Ford House Office Building
4th Floor, Second and D Streets SW, Washington, DC 20515

(202) 226-2602
e-mail: communications@cbo.gov
Web site: www.cbo.gov

The Congressional Budget Office was established by the Congressional Budget and Impoundment Control Act of 1974. Its mandate is to provide Congress with information, estimates, and objective analyses to aid in budgetary decisions. The CBO publishes studies and reports such as *Measuring the Effects of the Business Cycle on the Federal Budget*, as well as *Economic and Budget Issue Briefs*, a *Monthly Budget Review*, and Background Papers such as *Will the Demand for Assets Fall When the Baby Boomers Retire?*

Economic Policy Institute (EPI)
1333 H Street NW, Suite 300, East Tower
Washington, DC   20005
(202) 775-8810 • fax: (202) 775-0819
e-mail: epi@epi.org
Web site: www.epi.org

The Economic Policy Institute is a nonpartisan think tank that seeks to broaden economic policy debates to include the interests of low- and middle-income workers. It conducts research and informs and empowers citizens to demand an economic policy that provides prosperity and opportunity for all. The institute publishes the *EPI Journal*, as well as briefing papers, issue briefs, policy memoranda, and issue guides such as *Minimum Wage, Poverty and Family Budgets*, and *Welfare*.

Internal Revenue Service (IRS)
1111 Constitution Ave. NW, Washington, DC   20224
(800) 829-1040
Web site: www.irs.gov

The IRS is a bureau within the U.S. Treasury that facilitates and enforces citizens' compliance with U.S. tax law. It also provides information about compliance to federal, state, and local governments. The IRS publishes fact sheets, research bulletins, and annual data books.

National Priorities Project
243 King Street, Suite 239, Northampton, MA   01060
(413) 584-9556
Web site: www.nationalpriorities.org

National Priorities Project is a research organization that presents and analyzes federal budget data so that citizens can better understand how their tax dollars are spent. In addition to educating the public, the project collaborates with other groups on federal budget initiatives and facilitates dialogue between social justice and security policy groups. Its publications include the *Security Spending Primer*, fact sheets such as *Quick Facts About U.S. Military Operations in Afghanistan*, and many others.

Office of Management and Budget (OMB)
725 Seventeenth Street NW, Washington, DC   20503
(202) 395-3080 • fax: (202) 395-3504
Web site: www.whitehouse.gov/omb

The Office of Management and Budget is an Executive Branch office, the primary role of which is to assist the president in the preparation of the federal budget. The OMB also supervises the administration of the budget in the Executive Branch agencies. It publishes regular *OMB Bulletins* as well as news releases.

U.S. Department of Treasury
1500 Pennsylvania Ave. NW, Washington, DC   20220
(202) 622-2000 • fax: (202) 622-6415
Web site: www.treasury.gov

The U.S. Department of Treasury is the government agency responsible for promoting the nation's economic security and prosperity. The department advises the President, encourages economic growth, and facilitates the governance of financial institutions. It publishes press releases, fact sheets, and weekly wrap-ups.

U.S. Government Accountability Office (GAO)

441 G Street NW, Washington, DC   20548
(202) 512-3000
e-mail: contact@gao.gov
Web site: www.gao.gov

The Government Accountability Office is an independent non-partisan agency that works for the U.S. Congress. Its purpose is to investigate how federal tax dollars are spent and provide information to congressional committees and subcommittees. The GAO publishes regular reports on such topics as education spending and government operations.

Bibliography of Books

Donald L. Bartlett and James B. Steele — *The Great American Tax Dodge: How Spiraling Fraud and Avoidance Are Killing Fairness, Destroying the Income Tax, and Costing You.* New York: Little, Brown, 2000.

Scott Bittle and Jean Johnson — *Where Does the Money Go? Your Guided Tour to the Federal Budget Crisis.* New York: Harper, 2008.

Neal Boortz — *The FairTax Book.* New York: William Morrow, 2005.

Leslie Carbone — *Slaying Leviathan: The Moral Case for Tax Reform.* Dulles, VA: Potomac Books, 2009.

Pat Choate — *Saving Capitalism: Keeping America Strong.* New York: Vintage, 2009.

Jasmine Farrier — *Passing the Buck: Congress, the Budget, and Deficits.* Lexington, KY: University Press of Kentucky, 2004.

Steve Forbes — *Flat Tax Revolution: Using a Postcard to Abolish the IRS.* Washington, DC: Regnery, 2005.

John O. Fox — *If Americans Really Understood the Income Tax: Uncovering Our Most Expensive Ignorance.* New York: Basic Books, 2001.

Ellen Frank	*The Raw Deal: How Myths and Misinformation About the Deficit, Inflation, and Wealth Impoverish America.* Boston: Beacon, 2005.
William H. Gates Sr. and Chuck Collins	*Wealth and Our Commonwealth: Why America Should Tax Accumulated Fortune.* Boston: Beacon Press, 2003.
Michael J. Graetz	*100 Million Unnecessary Returns: A Simple, Fair, and Competitive Tax Plan for the United States.* New Haven, CT: Yale University Press, 2008.
Robert D. Hormats	*The Price of Liberty: Paying for America's Wars.* New York: Times Books, 2006.
Dennis S. Ippolito	*Why Budgets Matter: Budget Policy and American Politics.* University Park: Pennsylvania State University Press, 2003.
David Cay Johnston	*Perfectly Legal: The Covert Campaign to Rig Our Tax System to Benefit the Super Rich—and Cheat Everybody Else.* New York: Portfolio, 2003.
Paul R. Krugman	*The Great Unraveling: Losing Our Way in the New Century.* New York: W.W. Norton & Co., 2004.
Robert Kuttner	*Obama's Challenge: America's Economic Crisis and the Power of a Transformative Presidency.* White River Junction, VT: Chelsea Green, 2008.

Arthur B. Laffer, Stephen Moore, and Peter Tanous — *The End of Prosperity: How Higher Taxes Will Doom the Economy—If We Let It Happen*. New York: Threshold Editions, 2009.

Charles Lewis and Bill Allison — *The Cheating of America: How Tax Avoidance and Evasion by the Super Rich Are Costing the Country Billions—and What You Can Do About It*. New York: William Morrow, 2001.

Isaac Martin — *The Permanent Tax Revolt: How the Property Tax Transformed American Politics*. Palo Alto, CA: Stanford University Press, 2008.

Iwan Morgan — *The Age of Deficits: Presidents and Unbalanced Budgets from Jimmy Carter to George W. Bush*. Lawrence: University Press of Kansas, 2009.

David Osborne and Peter Hutchinson — *The Price of Government: Getting the Results We Need in an Age of Permanent Fiscal Crisis*. New York: Basic Books, 2006.

Peter G. Peterson — *Running on Empty: How the Democratic and Republican Parties Are Bankrupting Our Future and What Americans Can Do About It*. New York: Farrar, Straus and Giroux, 2004.

Alice M. Rivlin and Isabel V. Sawhill, eds. — *Restoring Fiscal Sanity: How to Balance the Budget*. Washington, DC: Brookings Institution Press, 2004.

| Allen Schick | *The Federal Budget: Politics, Policy, Process*, 3rd ed. Washington, DC: Brookings Institution Press, 2007. |

Joel Slemrod and Jon Bakija — *Taxing Ourselves: A Citizens Guide to the Debate over Taxes*, 4th ed. Cambridge, MA: MIT Press, 2008.

C. Eugene Steuerle — *Contemporary U.S. Tax Policy*. Washington, DC: Urban Institute Press, 2008.

Andrew L. Yarrow — *Forgive Us Our Debts: The Intergenerational Dangers of Fiscal Irresponsibility*. New Haven, CT: Yale University Press, 2008.

Index

moving beyond, 31–32
as necessary tool, 28–29, 30
Obama, Barack and, 30, 36–39
overview, 27–28
social security and, 35
Pell Grant funding, 107
Pelosi, Nancy, 51
Pence, Mike, 45–49
Penn, Schoen & Berland poll, 126
Perotti, Robert, 70
Pollin, Robert, 173–183
Prescription drug benefits, 188
PriceWaterhouse-Coopers study, 147
Private savings, 64
Prostitution tax, 147–148

Q

Quadrennial Defense Review (QDR), 165, 166

R

Reagan, Ronald (adminstration), 105, 182, 204
Reid, Harry, 51
Renewable energy spending, 176
Republican Party
bailouts and, 104
Department of Education and, 204
earmarks and, 46, 48–49, 53–54
fiscal responsibility and, 191
paternalism and, 196
politics of, 43, 160–161
Rubinomics and, 77
supplemental spending by, 41
tax cuts and, 75, 125
tax increases and, 124, 132

tax loopholes and, 129, 130
VAT and, 139
Reynolds, Alan, 67–72
Riedl, Brian M., 33–39, 110–111
Rivlin, Alice M., 26–32, 92–102
Rolling Stone (magazine), 59
Roosevelt, Franklin Delano, 58, 77, 149–150, 196
Rubin, Robert (Rubinomics), 68, 69, 72, 74–75, 77
de Rugy, Veronique, 40–44, 69, 103–107, 161
Rumsfeld, Donald, 54, 169

S

Sala-i-Martin, Xavier, 69
Samuelson, Robert J., 14, 60, 194
Sausalito, California, schools, 210–211
Savings, 64
Schaper, Donna, 118–122
Schiantarelli, Fabio, 70
Schifferes, Steve, 58
Scholastic Aptitude Test (SAT) scores, 208–209
Senate Appropriations Committee, 18, 169
Senate Budget Committee, 93, 187
Senate Finance Committee, 114, 143, 152, 187
September 11, 2009, attacks, 15, 125–126
Shays, Christopher, 169
Shrum, Robert, 50–55
Sin tax
alternatives to, 156–157
consequences of, 152–153
economic benefit of, 149–150